So, You Want to

So, You Want to be a Wrestling Promoter ?

Ric Drasin
with
Bruce Dwight Collins

ISBN 1-59109-949-8

To order additional copies, please contact us.
BookSurge, LLC
www.booksurge.com
1-866-308-6235
orders@booksurge.com

So, You Want to be a Wrestling Promoter ?

Introduction

Your palms are sweating, that nagging headache won't go away, you keep hearing loud boos and catcalls directed your way and you are not sure you can pay the twelve burly men at the end of the night. What are you ? Why, you're a pro wrestling promoter, of course.

The problem is, how did you get yourself in such a precarious position? I suspect you didn't read my book yet! If you don't act quick, the next snap, crackle and pop may not be your breakfast cereal!

Whether you are a promoter today or planning to be a promoter tomorrow, this is the book you've been waiting to read. Within these pages are valuable information for you to make wise choices to maximize profit, ease your mind and give you confidence that it is possible for you to create a wrestling event or operate a wrestling company.

This is actually two books in one with a wealth of promoting advice. First, my perspective and experience has been poured out into each chapter with many articles included, which were originally columns on wrestling websites, that I have updated. Second, the book *No Chicken Guts for the Wrestling Soul Revised* by Bruce Dwight Collins has been included for an added bonus.

I believe that with this knowledge, you will be able to formulate a plan of attack that will give you the edge to succeed. Nothing in life is guaranteed and obviously, there are many factors that determine outcomes but I believe there are two that far outweigh the rest and give you a distinct advantage. They are a positive attitude and knowledge.

I intend, through this book, to equip you with the knowledge and I hope that you develop a positive attitude. I have one and it has been invaluable in my success. It helps me as an actor, wrestler, father, husband and human being.

Most books are written without a sincere desire from the author for your success. Everyone that I have ever trained and everyone that I have ever offered my advice was done with a positive attitude and a belief that they could do it.

I also believe in you, for there is one thing that I know about you that you may not know. You want to succeed. You wouldn't have purchased this book unless there is something inside you that wants to feed your passion of this sport. That is step one.

Read this book, develop your plan and I hope to see you one day at your show.

-Ric

Introduction

Promoters in times past......

The world of the pro wrestling promoter has existed since the creation of modern day professional wrestling. The early displays of contemporary wrestling were performed during the heyday of the traveling carnival at the turn of the 19th to the 20th century. 'Promoters' or 'carneys' would find a suitable champion to tour from town to town while employing every method of keeping the belt on the insider.

Although challenges were solicited in the direction of the paying customer, the carney made sure that his champion would win. There are even stories of the champion purposely wrestling the challenger to the back so that someone could knock out the competitor with a wooden board. Also, the promoters encouraged their warriors to employ a method known as hooking, which simply meant that if the local was winning, the champion would use a hold to cripple the challenger (such as breaking an arm or leg).

In the early 1900's, the sport evolved into its' own entity. Wrestling shows were standing on their own feet and demanding their own marquee in halls and small auditoriums. Many prominent and successful early wrestlers were Ed "Strangler" Lewis, Frank Gotch, George Hackenschmidt, Gorgeous George, and Lou Thesz. Each of them had their own image (especially the flamboyant Gorgeous George).

Television brought the promoter a wider audience and wrestling was perfect for live television. Although today's version of professional wrestling is quite different than the mid-twentieth century style, television did allow wrestlers to connect with the audience through the interviews that were done in the ring and ringside. Most of the interviews in the early days were largely unpolished by today's standards.

Babyfaces (heroes) and heels (villains) were more prominent in those days. Many villains were Nazi sympathizers or foreigners from Communist countries (although their actual origins and accents were suspect). Promoters were already experimenting with how the audience could be manipulated into buying tickets by creating "heat" (fan reaction) to a wrestler's disposition or character.

Television during that time was a vehicle for the promoter to sell the live show. Although revenue was generated from television, live shows were the bread and butter of promotions.

Promoters were often as colorful as the wrestlers. Although every promoter had his own style, they were often eyed suspiciously by the wrestlers. In other words, many promoters have had a bad reputation since day one. As with most problems in life, the disputes often revolved around money. Promoters would lie about gate receipts and would try to hold on to an extra buck or two at a wrestler's expense. Every wrestler has a story along these lines.

As wrestling naturally evolved, so did the role of the promoter. Wrestlers who saw themselves getting too old to wrestle would often assume the role of promoter which would extend their time around the sport. Some of them were good businessmen and some were not.

Territories, as in regional promotions, began to form with a 'code of honor' that promotions would not infringe on the territories of other promotions. A wrestler could travel from region to region and find consistent work without over saturating his character in one town or state. Roy Shires operated in the San Francisco area, Verne Gagne in Minneapolis, Gene LeBelle in Los Angeles, Paul Boesch in Southern Texas, McMahon Sr. in the Northeast, the Crocketts in South Carolina, etc. Everyone had their piece of the wrestling pie.

A well known duo of promoters was the early team of Vince McMahon, Sr. and Toots Mondt, who formed the World Wide Wrestling Federation (WWWF) which was the birthing of the current World Wrestling Entertainment (WWE). The WWE is the current, dominant wrestling operation in North America. This was achieved when Vince, Sr., sold his empire to his son, Vince McMahon, jr., who had a vision of a national wrestling promotion. The WWE gobbled up many of the territorial operations. Some of those promoters went to work for Vince.

Today, wrestling holds less of the magic that it used to. Wrestling during the early to mid-twentieth century was treated with respect by the promoter and wrestler through "kayfabe". Kayfabe meant that the sport wouldn't divulge its' secrets from within. In other words, a heel and a babyface would not be seen outside of the ring together even if they really were friends due to the respect that each had with the 'illusion'. This is not the case with promoters or wrestlers today.

Ric Drasin would like to thank his wife, Randi, his sons, Adam and Shane, and daughter, Sami.

Chapter One

The type of Promoter you want to be....

The last chapter was written so that you could take a brief glimpse of our past. Take a look at it. Research it. It is important to know our roots. For one thing, I am a firm believer that this sport will return to its' roots one day. As you can see, promoters have always played a vital role in the life of wrestling. They, or you if you so choose, will play a role of equal importance in the future.

"The Equalizer" has spent his time in the ring. I've traveled thousands upon thousands of miles to appear in wrestling shows. I've shook the hands of countless fans and taken photos with hundreds. Decades in the ring have brought me face to face with all sorts of wrestlers.

I've also met a lot of promoters, too. There were the shifty ones and there were ones that I respected. I've seen some that would make you laugh and some that would make you want to knock their head clean off of their body. Sometimes it was the same promoter !

Let me say that from the outset I respect someone who has a dream. I respect someone who wants to prosper in professional wrestling. However, I cannot tolerate a cheat or charlatan promoter.

Why? Simply put, after years of being in the ring and years in front of the camera (whether wrestling or acting), I put my money where my mouth was and I entered the world of wrestling promotions. I started a company I call the American

Wrestling Federation. Whether or not the company has been successful (and it has-more on that later), I can say with a clear conscience that it is possible to be an upstanding, honest promoter.

I am one of them. I have never tried to cheat the competition. I have never tried to 'screw' the wrestlers. I have met numerous friends (such as my co-author, Bruce Collins) because I was always willing to lend a helping hand. That's how I conduct my business because that is how I behave. It is who I am, in and out of the ring.

So, regardless of what you will pick up from your competition, rule one of pro wrestling promoting is NOT to look for ways of cheating wrestlers and other promoters. Don't waste your time. Rise above it.

This book is written by experience. Experience will beat your underhandedness every time. Believe me, they've tried to stop "The Equalizer".

They didn't.

The first part of this book will be devoted to the basics such as the athletic commission and the beginnings of your business. I throw in some firsthand experiences as well as some history that I hope you will enjoy. The second half will be a glimpse into how I approach my wrestling school and other aspects of this profession.

I believe this will not only be a unique book about promoting but it will be very thorough so that you will feel like "The Equalizer" is right there in your corner.

I am.

Chapter Two

Wrestling's big brother: The Athletic Commission....

The athletic commission has been a part of wrestling since the beginning. The New York Athletic Commission was the one that recognized such champions as Ed "Strangler" Lewis when he defeated Jack Sherry in 1910. Why wouldn't the athletic commission look over the sport in the early 20th century? Look at the following newspaper article in the *Chicago Sunday Tribune* on November 30, 1913 and you can see that wrestling was treated as 100% legitimate.

> Lewis has been dubbed "Strangler" Lewis by those who follow the mat sport, but not because of the "neck yoke," as might be supposed. When he was in the primer of wrestling he gained some little fame by applying the original strangle hold to his opponents, and this, together with the fact that one of the most famous mat men the world ever knew was named "Strangler" Lewis, was responsible for the handle attached to his name. The history of the sport tells plenty about the original "Strangler," Evan Lewis.
> Although Lewis has really been in the game only about two years, he spent a great deal of his time experimenting on the hold which now promises to make him famous. He had gained a considerable knowledge of the regulation holds which are applied

when the men are on the mat, and he set about to discover tactics that would give him an advantage while he was contesting with an opponent head to head in an effort to gain a grip that would bring an opponent to the floor on the defensive. He discovered the neck yoke, which he calls a neck or head lock. First he tried the play for the hold with his right arm, but changed to the left when he discovered he could apply greater leverage that way.

You can see why the athletic commission kept a strong hold on professional wrestling. There were several reasons but among them was the safety of athletes, recognizing champions (keeping things official) as well as collecting fees. It might be logical for some government body to keep an eye on a 'strangler'!

As time has passed and wrestling has changed so has the athletic commission. The hold that the commission has on the sport is different from state to state. When you are ready to take the journey of pro wrestling promotions, take a visit to your state's government websites. Search for the athletic commission and see if they still regulate professional wrestling. States such as New York, Nevada, South Carolina and Nebraska still operate in the grip of the AC. Nevada has a stiff license fee of $5,000 so that alone will be a tough expense for the small business promoter.

We are fortunate in California because the AC is not regulating pro wrestling shows. That could change. In fact, there are rumblings that it will. This prompted me to write the following column on www.americanwrestlingfederation.com:

When the Athletic Commission was in Force!

A decade ago there was a force known as the State Athletic Commission. They had jurisdiction over Boxing Events and Pro Wrestling Events. The commission had good points and bad points about them. It was not unlike Screen Actors Guild of today for Actors.

You had to be licensed through them in order to wrestle or

you didn't work. If they were in force today, about 90% of the local wrestlers would not be working.

I'll tell you why. There were very strict rules to become a Wrestler. Like I said, you had to be licensed through the State of California, which meant you had to have a physical from a commission Dr., eye test, blood test, chest x-ray, fingerprints (police) background check and a fee of $20. Sounds pretty simple if you meet the criteria. But not only that, you also had to have a booking date and it had to be through a State of California Promoter who was licensed through the state.

A Promoter's License was even harder to get. Not only did you have a $500 fee for the license, but also you had to post a bond of "$5000.00' and provide 2 Million dollar liability insurance, have a steady venue that was specifically made for Wrestling. There had to be funds to insure payment to wrestlers and then a load of paper work before each show with every 'licensed' wrestler listed, ticket sales,etc. Tickets had to be attained through a specific ticket company which was ok'd by the commission and numbered in sequence and counted before and after each show by a representative from the commission. I had to get a promoter's license in my wife's name so that I could wrestle. You couldn't hold two different licenses.

They would show up at every match, check your license have a Dr. on hand to check your blood pressure and health and if you didn't pass or have a license you couldn't work. The commission also collected a % of ticket sales at the end of every event for the state. Paper work had to be in their office 5 days prior to any show with all changes or you couldn't run.

If there was another promotion in town which then was not considered 'Indy' but opposition or 'outlaw promotion', the commission did everything they could to make it tough on them to run a show and scrutinized all the paper work and sometimes at the last minute wouldn't let them run.

Since Vince McMahan declared Wrestling under the terms of Entertainment he got the commission debarred in some states, Calif. being one of them. But, by doing that he also exposed the business for what it is today. Back then there was still a certain mystery about it being real or not. No one really went behind the 'Kafabe'. Even the commission was in the dark about it. Today as you know, everyone knows the 'high spots' and finishes. Too bad cause who wants to really know the secrets of wrestling or magic. It's much more fun to wonder as through a 'kid's eyes.

When I say the commission compared to the Screen Actors Guild, I meant that you just couldn't join SAG. YOU have to have a film or commercial lined up through a Producer that needs your type and sends a letter to SAG for you to join. Otherwise you can't get in. You need to be a member to work and you can't get work unless you're a member. This was how wrestling was then. It wasn't flooded with unskilled talent like today and people who claim they're wrestlers after 3 lessons.

To get a license back then you really had to know how to work and be approved by the promoter.

There was a rumor that came passed me about a month ago that the commission was going to be back in force. Now it may just be a rumor but if it comes to pass, all the old rules will apply again and you can see where that will lead. They still have a commission in many places such as Oregon and Nevada and they are very strict in those areas. Remember the State wants all it's tax money from every source. Wrestling is 'hot'. They got it before and they'll try to get it again. Especially now that wrestling is in the spotlight.

Be thankful that you can work today the way it is. But on the other hand maybe it's better that it should be limited to those who qualify.

Chapter Three

Wrestling has a style.....

Whether you are talking about wrestling today or wrestling in the past, there is a style attached to it. Both types of wrestling have their own share of fans. The younger fans today like the fast paced version that is being aired on television. At least, they think they like it. There aren't many alternatives for them to see the old style of wrestling.

If they did, they might change their minds. In my mind, the old style was much more realistic.

As a promoter, you may want to start your fans with a mixture of both styles. It keeps things more entertaining and you appeal to every age group and taste. When I promote and wrestle on the same show, my match is the old style and the fan reaction is great.

Before we talk about taking action on your new career as promoter, let's study the differences between wrestling today and yesterday.

Old School Wrestling vs. Today's Wrestling

I remember when I was a kid, my Dad saying to me how much things were better in the old days. I never quite knew what he meant until I became older and looked back in retrospect. It's true, cars were more classic and built with much more care and detail. Homes were built with real plaster, not drywall. Communities were safer, families were more together, movies had more meaning and left a lot to your imagination, etc., and speaking of imagination, there is not much left in wrestling today.

Today everyone is a critic, knowing what spots are called, the finishes, who's going over and who missed what spot during a match. When I was a kid, we just went to the wrestling matches and enjoyed them and went home. We didn't critique each move and analyze each person and what they did in the ring. We just knew there were bad guys and good guys and had fun.

I was trained 'Old School Style' and to this day believe that it was so much better and much more enjoyable to watch. You had to know how to sell, use holds, actually 'wrestle' and the wrestlers back then were NOT called 'Workers' even though it was a 'work'. They were called **Wrestlers** and they looked the part. Each guy was unique and if you spotted him on the street, you just knew he was a wrestler! He had the look. Kayfabe was BIG. We couldn't even ride to the matches together and if we did, one of us had to get out of the car 3 blocks away so that the fans wouldn't see us together. We couldn't even socialize in public. Even though people thought it was *fake*, they weren't sure! Everything in the ring looked solid, and high spots were used sparingly. There were maybe 2 or 3 during a match. The rest were submission holds and takedowns. It was much more believable than today's wrestling. Ring psychology was very important. Something you don't see today at all. If you were working your opponent's arm, he sold it to the end. You could swear that it was hurt and unusable. Less was 'more'. Too many moves in a match became confusing. It's similar to a movie with nothing but car chases (high spots) and very little story line. Today when you work someone, they make a comeback and sell nothing. Punches were used sparingly, but when you did use them, they looked like they connected and did the job. Today, punches are mostly openhanded to the head, which does nothing, and you'll see at least 10 to 20 during a match that do nothing and are not sold at all. If you were really going to punch someone, would you punch him in the head?? No, I don't think so, you'd break your hand. You have to think logically what is believable and what isn't. The fans have been re-educated to expect what they see today and the more you give them the more they expect or they get bored.

But, if you are convincing and use 'old school' psychology, you re-educate them and make them believe this is real! That's what we are out there to do! Somehow that notion has been getting lost. Todays younger wrestlers think it's all about risky high spots (like Mick Foley) and that's what gets them over. Might as well just do movie stunts if you think that way cause there is no skill involved to do that, just plain risky stupidity. That's why there are so many injuries and deaths.

Some of the 'old school' matches were so believable that even the boys in the locker room thought that it was a shoot. We carried it right into the dressing room and let it cool down for 10 min before we even talked. This is what the fans saw also and they were never quite sure if it was real or not. Look at Andy Kaufman and Jerry Lawler. They pulled off the biggest work of all cause they carried it to the max! That was definitely Old School psychology.

Today, everyone hangs out together with the fans and are buddy buddy, the fans know as much as the guys in the ring as far as what is going on. Most Indy wrestlers look like high school kids, with no builds to speak of and wrestle in jeans and shirts, which cover any exposed flesh that would make them look like an athlete. Old School wrestlers wore trunks and boots and looked the part.

The fans today in the Indy scene especially are what you call 'arm chair critics' and basically 'bash' every wrestler in the ring as if they could do better. Most are overweight little marks that would crumble in the ring if you got them in there. Years ago, if one of them came in the ring during a match, they were literally sent out on a stretcher. Today they get away with being part of the show.

There was no Internet back then which in one way is bad, as it could have helped promoted many shows. But in other ways, everyone has access to message boards and writes obscene reviews of these wrestlers and shows and trashes the 'boys' who work hard in the ring to become something. I even read where one wrestler thanked another on the message board for putting him over and taking all the bumps for him. This is the sort of thing that destroys the business. The sad thing is that some people read this and believe it not knowing that it came from some 16 year old punk sitting behind his computer at home with absolutely no knowledge or skill of wrestling or what it takes to be one.

If you want to people to believe that you are a wrestler, then you better be proud of the fact and not let them think that you are a fake! You have to carry the Kayfabe around and make them believers. That's what draws an audience. You want people to walk away and say, that was one tough SOB.

I have seen so many movies that I like and have read trash about from so called film critics who didn't like it. I could never understand their power of keeping people from going to a good movie. By the same token these wrestling critics can do the same thing with what they write. In both cases, if all these people are such experts, then why don't they come up with the perfect film or the perfect wrestler and match? Makes sense to me.

But, if you get the average family out there to watch, they don't critique a match, they just sit and enjoy it and go home.

So, in my estimation, if you watch old tapes of wrestling from the 60's and 70', you will see that the matches were much more believable. No, they didn't have the glitz and lighting and modern day technology, but they were a great show and you were never quite sure if it was a shoot or not.

Today, it's mainly microphone work, some quick high spots and it's over. It's become basically boring. In many cases, some of the Indy wrestlers want to run their own shows. That's a good idea as it will create more interest in the business, but most of them don't take the time to learn how to promote it. They run a show, very little advertising and end up drawing 20 people. Not enough to even pay expenses let alone the 'boys'. This gets frustrating and pretty soon no one wants to work, as there is no audience. In this case, they should have capital to run, plan out their advertisement, get some TV spots and then build a card.

I've been training some of these people and have demonstrated the use of old school technique along with today's methods and they seem to understand and are having much better matches because of it.

Everything in life goes around full cycle. So, eventually 'Old School' will return and the matches will be much better!

Chapter Four

Think like the Equalizer...

There are many ways to promote a show. There are also many ways to lose money. I have developed a way for you to maximize profit and minimize risk. I am a firm believer of the wrestling fundraiser. It's a perfect arrangement because you make a club or charity happy in the process.

Obviously, you are not going to become a millionaire overnight in this profession. Don't quit your day job! However, I am living proof that you can make money as a promoter. Do lots of research during this time.

Contact every local school and charity to set up a fundraiser. If they have never done this before, they may be suspicious of the reputation of wrestling. In other words, you have to reassure them that the action will not spill into the audience, that equipment will not be damaged and that the wrestlers will be on their best behavior. You are the promoter and you have to convey that you are in control of the situation.

You must always brainstorm. Think of new ideas to market your product. Some ideas you will throw to the curb but others will be vital to your success. You will grow your business as your mind and creative thoughts grow.

Here is an easy 1,2,3 plan to get your promoting experience started:

Starting Your Own Federation

So, you've decided to become a Wrestling Promoter and start your own Federation. Well, where do you begin? It's not as easy as it looks or more people would be successful at it. First of all, there is NOT a whole lot of money in it. Most promoters lose money and some if lucky, just break even.

I'm sure your have heard the horror stories about wrestlers not getting paid after a show, or the Promoter ducking out before anyone can find him or the plane tickets never arrived. This is so common in this business that it ruins it for everyone involved.

Being a Wrestler is easy. You just have to show up. Many of the boys ask me when I'm going to run another show. Well, a few years ago, I had many and they were easier to line up. Lately I think that Wrestling has become over saturated and the interest on the Indy level has declined. Going into a building and putting up a ring and hoping people show, is way too risky. If you draw 100 people you are really lucky. The biggest problem is 'promotion'. Letting people know you are there, is so important. ***If no one knows, no one shows!*** You need a good plan.

First of all, you must have access to Wrestlers. You need to have at least 30 on a list in case some can't show and you need stand by matches. Plus, you should find out the reputation of your talent and see if they are reliable. You don't want someone to commit to being there and then not show after you have advertised them.

You will need a Ring obviously. If you don't have one, you can rent one and the price should be fair. No more than $350 for the night. You will also want to list all the people that you need to work the event.

Lighting
Camera
Ticket Booth
Door Man
Security
Time Keeper
Referee
Dressing Room Monitor (send guys out etc.)
Announcer
These are basics and mostly you can get friends to do it

for 'free' admission. The building if you rent it, should cost, no more than $500.

Liability Insurance is another thing. You don't want to get sued by someone who gets hurt. I carry 2 Million Dollar liability. I have a blanket coverage that costs me $180.00 a year for show, training people, etc. If I have to additionally insure a **venue**, it's an added $35 for the night. That is very reasonable and necessary.

Now your overhead with paying 12 wrestlers ($50) each will be around the $1200.00 mark, give or take. I haven't figured in publicity at this point. I always make posters and flyers and leave them all over the area where I am running a show. I will also get our radio stations here to plug it. Sometimes that's difficult but in my case I have a lot of friends that are DJs. Same with some of the local News Channels. This is just an added plus.

In order to make a profit at this point, you will need in attendance 120 people at $10 a head. Ok, it goes up from there. Also figure in that kids prices will be cheaper at maybe $6. This increases the number you need to attend.

Now, the best way to do this rather than taking a risk on a building is to find a club or charity or in my case I use a high school and get the PE Dept. to sponsor it. I ask for a $2,000 dollar deposit and then we do a 50/50 split on profits at the door. My $2000 is deducted on my 50% at that point. Having the club or school involved assures me that they will help promote by giving flyers out to every student (1000 or 2000) and that a good number of those kids will show up and bring their family and friends. Last time I did this, I had 600 people show up and it was a big success.

I give the school concessions as part of the incentive. I also tell the wrestlers to bring photos , t shirts, and anything that they want to sell.

Having that deposit also guarantees me payment for the ring, wrestlers and all other expenses and includes my profit.

At the show, I already have everyone's payment, (in cash) in an envelope with his or her name on it. I want everyone to go home happy! I send out booking agreements and after the show

I include with payment a letter of thanks for their participation. I feel it's important to treat everyone as a professional and with respect. Having wrestled for years, I have been on all ends of that and I want everyone to know that I respect him or her.

One week prior to a show, I do a personal appearance at the school and bring a few wrestlers to a pep rally to get the school charged up to attend the event. This works really well.

I also will send a letter of thanks to the School or charity that we worked for thanking them for the help and asking to schedule another show for the following year. After doing this quite a few times, you can usually keep yourself booked throughout the whole next year.

This is a good formula to follow and it works. Remember, you just don't throw up a ring in a building like a 'backyard fed' and expect it to work.

Think it through, plan it out and then work your plan.

Much success to you all!

Chapter Five

TRAINING FOR PRO WRESTLING

I was watching TV last night when WWF's Tough Enough came on. It was interesting to see how they narrowed down 4000 video entries to 220 people and then down to 25 and on to 13. I pretty much picked the same people they did. They spoke of personality, charisma and athletic ability along with a good physique.

All these things are important but most important is the Charisma. As Al Snow said, you either have it or you don't. I've been saying this for years. It's something from within you at birth. You can't develop it.

Well, with the 13 that they have, they will narrow it down to two people who may get a contract with WWF, a man and a woman. Their method is a little different than most when it comes to training and I think it's purposely intended for a TV viewing audience.

Humiliation, rolling in mud, odd exercises, etc. I did none of these when I started out and I don't know anyone else who did either. Most were trained in a ring privately from a current or former wrestler, who showed them the holds, moves and ring psychology. Not once did I have to be drilled like boot camp or go through those antics.

I guess it's good TV, but realistically that doesn't need to take place. I've trained Men, Women and Kids and my methods have always worked. I just took it upon myself to train 10 Hollywood Actresses between the ages of 20 and 30 to use on some shows and also do some Women's wrestling videos. These girls came to me with absolutely no experience at all other than acting.

I felt that if I kept 8 that were focused, I could do something with them. Now, we're not thinking of WWF but movie, commercial and TV work. There is a lot of work available for wrestlers and also female wrestler which there is a shortage of. And, I do get calls as a stunt coordinator to find those qualified. That's when I decided to qualify some myself and train them.

I start them out with drills of rolls, back rolls, running ropes, running into a handstand and a forward bump, back bumps, leap frogs, etc. Then we center in on holds, reversals, takedowns, some shoot holds, and high spots. All along I teach them ring and crowd psychology and tell them that there is a reason for everything that they do in the ring. Don't do anything that isn't logical or doesn't make sense. Learn how to control a crowd with emotions. I also stress that all this can be used on acting auditions, as it's great practice to work in front of people. Besides that when you add Pro Wrestling to your resume, it keeps you in the audition longer cause everyone wants to talk about it and not a lot of people have that experience. So, it's good in that respect also.

Teaching them made me look at myself and how much I've learned over the years and now pass it on. But in the process, I'm also re learning again cause you take the time to show how to execute holds, and possible escapes. It's great training and great teaching and learning for all of us. I told them not to be impatient that it takes months to get it right and learn the proper way, but it would also bring out their personality and they will learn a lot about themselves. It's already happening. I can see a difference in less than a month.

I won't have them run through the mud, or humiliate them like the Tough Enough show is doing, as it's not necessary for this. However it is interesting to watch on TV and it's necessary for the new trend of reality shows.

I also tape these sessions and show their progression and

who knows, maybe someday I'll have enough tape to edit and show the making of Ric's Women of Wrestling.

I have also started a summer wrestling camp for kids from ages 10 to 17 to teach them the proper way of ring work without hurting themselves and others. Also self respect and respect for their friends. I think this will boost self-esteem and hopefully stop some of them from hurting each other in back yard wrestling feds.

It's nice to do something good for the community and there is a great deal of satisfaction in doing so.

Chapter Six

Self Promotion and Re-Inventing Yourself For Wrestling, Bodybuilding, Acting or Work

In any business, you must have a game plan. You must have a way of exploiting your product and calling attention to it via making it different than any other product around. In this case we are talking about you.

If you walk into a store and a salesperson helps you, that person can either make or break the sale. In this world there are those people who *'know'* or those who *'don't know'*. In most cases, it's those who *don't know*. We see them everyday in Malls, Supermarkets, and on the Freeways. They haven't got a clue what they are doing or what life is about but they seem to get by somehow. I haven't figured out how, but they do it.

You want to be in the category of those *who 'know'*. I have 3 children, two boys Shane 19 , Adam 22 and a daughter Sami ,9. All 3 of them since birth are in the category of those who *'know'*. You can see it in their eyes. They can spot a situation and just know if it's right or not. I can see in their eyes whether they understand something or not and in every case, they have always caught on.

I was explaining something the other day to someone about laying out a CD cover design and the steps involved. I could see in his eyes as I was explaining that he just didn't get it. He said he did, but his eyes said something else. I think they said, 'duh'!

So, I told him, you really don't understand do you. He said, 'not exactly'. I knew that right off. I told him about re-inventing and coming up with an entirely different look on his CD. It's like when you listen to a record, if the song doesn't catch you in the first 5 sec. you move on. It's the same thing with a look or a visual. It has to catch your eye.

So, when you are promoting yourself, you want people to look at you as the person who 'knows'. It'll emit from you if you have it.

Self-promotion in Acting or Wrestling for example means creating a persona that everyone will notice and set you apart from the others. You can see a crowd of people and maybe one person in that crowd will catch your eye. Could be their looks, usually is, but it goes beyond that and it comes from something within them. It's body language and a feeling that they know who they are and what they are portraying. That's considered 'Star quality'.

I go on film and commercial auditions with a lot of different types of people. I have several categories that I fit in and let's take one for example. Bikers. Lots of people show up dressed like bikers and some are pretty authentic looking. But on camera, if they don't have it inside of them, it won't come across as real or as what they are trying to be. They just don't 'know'.

You have to have charisma. That is something that you usually have or not have. It's very hard to develop but can be developed to a small degree if you work on your persona and attitude.

Ever see a really pretty girl and when you finally talk to her, she's dead as far as personality? Well, that is persona and at that point, the beauty really means nothing.

When I was younger and going out on commercials, the look I had was with hair and mustache. I looked very similar to Tom Selleck. Many of the actors that I went to auditions had taken on the same look. However I was able to come across on camera better as my personality came through at the right moment and I booked 5 National Cigarette Ads and 4 National Beer commercials. I was bodybuilding and in really good shape but didn't show it off blatantly as it would have been too much. But a plaid shirt with the sleeves rolled up and jeans did the job and showed a little muscle. This was something that a lot of the others didn't have. It made me look more like the outdoor type that did hard labor.

So, I was on to something. Just keep re-inventing my look from time to time and stay ahead of the pack.

In music and advertising, you always have to come up with something new and fresh that hasn't been seen. This is what sells. Well, the same thing goes for you. If you want to be an actor, then you need to find a slot that isn't filled and make yourself be seen.

It's the same thing with wrestling. Years ago in the 50's and 60's, wrestlers had entirely different looks. Each one was really unique. Not all were muscular but different sizes and shapes, but they DID look like wrestlers. Gorgeous George bleached his hair blonde before all the others and made a huge name for himself. Pretty soon others followed, Ray Stevens, Pat Patterson, Billy Graham, Hulk Hogan, etc. But it started somewhere. Today, pretty much all the wrestlers look the same and all are bodybuilders. It was the same way with bodybuilding. Arnold, Draper, Zane, Katz, Colombu all looked different. Entirely different body shapes and size and it made a contest interesting. Look at today's bodybuilder. I can't tell one from the other. They all look exactly the same. There is nothing different or unique about them.

When I designed the Gold's Gym logo with the little 'bald headed' weightlifter, I said, one day, that will be my look-! It was about 15 years later that I decided to finally shave my head. I kept telling my wife that I was going to do it and it would create a whole new avenue for acting and wrestling. Ten years ago, I shaved it and grew my goatee. Very few people, if any had that look. I loved the look and wish I would have done it years before. Before I knew it, I was booking more films and commercials than ever. The *look* worked and created a whole new persona for me. Little by little I saw others showing up on auditions with shaved heads and beards. Hmm, I thought, this is catching on and catching up with me. It's time to re-invent again. So, two years ago, I bleached my beard and mustache white with two brown side stripes. It was unusual and no one else at this point will copy me because I have established it as MY LOOK and people know me by that. As my motto goes, ' Often Imitated, but Never Duplicated'.

Well, I got more work and more compliments on the look. Sure it stands out, but that's what I want. It sets me aside from the others. I have offered to color it for TV jobs with a roux stick which is temporary simply because some sponsors may want it dark or all white, but in every case, they wanted to leave it as it is.

I used to get asked on auditions if I would shave it off for a commercial. In my younger years, I would have agreed reluctantly, but now I say a definite NO. I tell them, it's my look, you called me in because you obviously like it, so why would you want me to shave it off and then maybe you won't like me without it? There are plenty of guys in the waiting room without beards, take one of them. Plus, if I shave it off and have another audition tomorrow, it'll knock me out of a job.

I love standing up for myself. The production companies respect that and I get the job. It just lets them know that they can't walk all over you. Also, what you have created works for you.

Now, with wrestling, it's the perfect look. I go out on a lot of auditions calling for a Wrestler. I see bodybuilders there, fat guys, skinny guys, etc. mostly actors and not many wrestlers. But, not many have the look. I make sure that I show up in tights, boots, etc. and I take my championship belt. That's a big plus and has cinched many jobs. It's just an added feature and prop that the production companies don't have to think about.

I was called out on a FLOOZ commercial that aired this year and they brought me in with some bodybuilders. I came in my wrestling wear and suggested that why not change the character to a wrestler instead of a bodybuilder. It's much more popular and more alive. They took my suggestion and I landed the national spot.

So, there again, I created a character that works. Plus in this case it helps to know how to wrestle, even if you don't use it, as they may want a few holds, etc.

I have tried one more thing recently. I made my beard all white for some pictures and put on some wire frame glasses and a judge's robe. I took a few shots behind a courtroom desk with a gavel. It was a perfect picture to play a judge and I had noticed that there are many roles on TV for judges. I gave these pictures to my agent and he has begun submitting me on those roles.

I always have set my own style in clothes and I had my own clothing line for years in Muscle & Fitness Magazine, called Big Boy Wear. I like to dress different, but with taste and many people come up to me and compliment me on what I'm wearing. Well, it suits me and I make it work, but it's because I feel secure with myself and I like to be creative. It works for me.

A lot of the independent wrestlers today copy each other with what they wear in the ring. I can't tell them apart. Every once in awhile someone will enter the ring with a unique outfit. Well, it stands out and gets attention.

Take a good look at yourself and write down ideas that you see for yourself in the future. If it's acting, bodybuilding, wrestling or even outside sales, you need a persona. Find what works for you and develop it. When it gets to the point that it goes stale and/or doesn't work any longer, re-invent again.

One person comes to mind as he had 50 different album covers and never looked the same in any one of them. David Bowie. I saw a documentary on him and how he kept going through the re-invention process and it started me on my way. It works, try it. Remember, you want to be one of those, who 'know.'

Chapter Seven

You're a promoter, why should you respect kayfabe ?

There is no doubt that everyone knows all about wrestling. The business has been exposed, re-exposed, looked at upside down and sideways but I believe that the old rules should still apply. Kayfabe was a 'secret word' used in the business way back in the 50's. When an outsider would enter a room where you were talking over your match with another wrestler, someone would yell 'kayfabe' which meant 'shut up' and go about your business, not to leak out any information. It's a great 'word' and can be used in many situations.

I believe that kayfabe will give your business an extra edge. Why? Think about other forms of entertainment where there is a trick or two performed in front of an audience. The audience wants to be amazed. They want to wonder how it is done. They don't want to be reminded that a magician is 'fake'. It's not necessary and actually, it's damaging to the illusion. I wouldn't want to know the actual secrets of magic unless I was going to perform them. It'd take the fun away and make it look too easy.

Now, pro wrestling might not be able to get its' old image back. We may not be able to reverse the damage that has been done but we can at least suspend reality for our fans.

Let me give you an example.

Two wrestlers on your show Saturday night had a brutal fifteen minute match. It seemed to go back and forth until finally someone got the pin.

On Monday morning, the 'heel' posts on your message

board (on the internet) that he was really proud of the match on Saturday. He felt that they really gave a great 'performance' for the fans and that they didn't screw up at all. This exposes the business and the Internet "Marks' have been famous for doing that.

Instead of exposing the match as fake, he should have written that they had a great match, that his opponent really gave him a run for his money and that there were times he didn't think he'd win. Now, that's SELLING the match. More people will be interested in a rematch. If nothing is written, even better. Let the mystery become a bigger mystery. The key to this is selling. So many wrestlers have not learned the art of selling and what it means to a match. That's what makes it believable. If you don't sell, you give no credibility to your opponent and visa versa. Do not hang out with your opponent and sit out in the seats with him after your match to watch the show. This destroys the whole idea of Kayfabe.

Do you see the difference? Despite the fact that people know what they know, promoters are still in the business of creating interest in the product.

Also, if you are out of town and promoting a wrestling show, you should encourage the heels and faces not to eat or socialize with each other in public. This is having respect for your audience. It is traditional.

Wrestlers and promoters should sell everything. When a wrestler walks back to the curtain, he shouldn't stroll, he should be selling whatever damage was done to him. Promoters should sell on the internet and in interviews. If heels post messages, they should sell that they are rude and obnoxious.

When a wrestler is coming in from out of town and he will be facing your superstar, you don't want to say that he is a good worker and you think he will work well with your champion. You want to say that this wrestler has been unbeatable in the past but your ring warrior has been unstoppable, also. That's why the fans better not miss it because there is no telling who is going to win.

Also, if those two wrestlers are in an interview, they don't want to be civil to each other, they want to throw down the challenge. Kayfabe has to be consistent. The fans have to get used to it again and they have to know you won't take away the illusion.

Years ago even the wrestler's family were not in on the business end of wrestling. They kept a Kayfabe at home and it wasn't even discussed. This is the way it should be!

Kayfabe still works. I recommend it.

Chapter Eight

WHAT IS A MARK?

In essence, we are all 'Marks' in some form. When we go to a movie, aren't we marks for the film and the actors? We know it's not real and it's special effects, but we are taken in by the story and the visual and we want to believe that it's real for those two hours of sitting.

What about Football, Basketball, Baseball? Those people are called 'fans', but aren't they really 'Marks?" I think so! What about Concerts with Rock Groups? There are 'fans' and there are 'groupies." But are they 'Marks?" Yep!

Anytime we are involved in something of interest and we are a 'Fan' of it, we are a 'Mark' in some form.

There are people who admire Policemen, Firemen, Military, etc. These people hero worship to some degree to fulfill their dreams as it's something that maybe they wanted to do with their lives.

There is really nothing wrong with that. Marks are die-hard fans that will fight for you and defend you and build your self-esteem and promote you. In every sport and in wrestling, you need marks. These are the mainstay of any business. They are the supporters and without them, you have nothing.

Now here's another little tidbit. I guarantee you that every wrestler that you see today on TV, with the WWF or any other federation at one time prior was a "Mark" -Triple H, Steve Austin, Big Show, etc., etc. They were all 'marks.' They just didn't decide one day to become a Wrestler. They had to grow up watching it, getting involved, having favorites, and then pursued it and made it a reality. They all had someone that they looked up to and developed their style from that person.

It says right on Superstar Graham's website that he was in 'awe' of Pat Patterson and his work as a heel and how he could piss off the fans. He patterned his work after him. So, basically he was a 'mark' for Pat.

Then you have the 'Internet Marks' who just sit at their computers and hack away at tearing everyone down. I don't consider these real 'marks.' These are more destructive people who like to pass time just rambling and creating chaos with little to no knowledge of the business. Most of them are children or teenagers who have no perspective of the business over any lasting period of time. They can't appreciate tradition or the roots of wrestling. They don't do the business any good other than it keeps wrestlers names out there. Good or Bad publicity doesn't matter as long as people are talking about you.

A good example of a bad mark is the Robert Duvall character in the classic baseball movie," The Natural". His character wrote about baseball the way he saw it. It was an egotistical, arrogant view that was so narcissistic that he felt he was actually 'creating' baseball the way it should be created and portrayed. It's that type of attitude from someone with little or no experience in the actual sport that is so troubling. They are trying to shape it but in the process, they are ruining it.

But as I said, the Internet wrestling marks are destructive. It's the real ringside 'marks' that help the business.

The word 'Mark' is from the Carney Business or Carnival as you know it. Barkers or people at booths try to rope you in to hit the 3 dolls with a baseball. Making you believe you can do it. They consider you a mark, or a sucker for the business they sell you.

Wrestling originated in the Carney as a sideshow. They either had two wrestlers or people from the audience wrestle their wrestler. The audience person was planted there and no one knew the difference. OF course they were all 'marks' watching. They were believers in what was going on.

So, today when we work a show and we see the marks, we are only trying to sell to them our story and make them believers. We want them there, and we want to convince them of what we do is real. Remember that and next time you call someone a 'mark', shake their hand and thank them for their support.

We, the wrestlers and promoters, should respect them enough to tell the story in the ring and to promote kayfabe and the fans, in turn, should respect our profession.

Now, take a look inside of you. What are you a 'mark' for? Huuuhhhh?

Chapter Nine

An Indy Promoter can learn from the national promotions

Once you have deep roots in the wrestling business, you have to maintain your hold on your fanbase.

Wrestling has always been about wrestling and entertainment. The entertainment complimented the wrestling but the emphasis was definitely on wrestling. Today, it is vice versa. Not only did the balance between wrestling and entertainment change but the style of the entertainment is different. In the past, it was more of a carnival atmosphere. Today, it is a lot like an episode of Jerry Springer.

As I said before, kayfabe should be an important part of your operations. There are many ways to respect kayfabe. One way is to employ good wrestlers. Too many poorly trained wrestlers do not even know the basics. They can't even throw a decent punch. How can you have kayfabe without a degree of believability in the ring?

I think the wrestlers should also try to look like wrestlers. Boxers do not dress in ripped shirts and beat up denim. Wrestlers should look the part. The only one to have cut off jeans in the ring better have a name that starts with Haystacks or Hillbilly. What happened to the robes and capes that once adorned wrestlers?

Pro wrestlers should look better dressed, be more muscular and better trained than the audience.

Managers could still work in wrestling. Many indy

managers are poorly trained. They shouldn't try to take heat away from the match. When there is a lull in the action and the two wrestlers are on the mat, that's when the manager maintains the heat directed at the heel by firing up the crowd.

There are no managers on a national scale. Only female valets join the wrestlers at ringside. None of them are over. They are simply eye candy. Once their beauty begins to fade and a new, young girl comes along, they will be quickly forgotten yet nobody will forget Bobby "The Brain" Heenan. That's the difference.

Use managers in the indy ranks as long as they heed the words of the Rock. Know your role.

Another thing that I do not understand about modern televised wrestling is how they are using promos. Wrestlers now walk to the ring, not to wrestle, but to grab a microphone and talk. Then, the other guy they are talking about brings a microphone out to the ramp and talks back to him. Not only is this not believable but it is ruining some of their reputations.

A perfect example is a current superstar in the WWE. When he had a manager who spoke for him, he looked like a menacing heel. He kept quiet and let his sneer, massive muscles and ring work do the talking. His push in wrestling at such an early phase in his career came from the fear in his total imagery. Now, Brock Lesnar is doing his own promos which make him look like a babyface with his soft spoken voice and he may have permanently destroyed his gift of intimidation.

The story needs to be told in the ring by the wrestling. If you must advance the story through mic work, then have a ring announcer stop the wrestler after a match to interview him. If the 'heel' would destroy himself by speaking, you could have it go something like this:

Ring Announcer," Equalizer, what are you going to do to Fred Ray when you get him in the ring next week?"

Instead of the Equalizer going on and on, he grabs the ring announcer by the tie and pushes him. Then he walks off with a mean look on his face.

You just told the story with little dialogue. The ring

announcer hyped the next match and the Equalizer stayed in character. Doesn't that make sense?

That's how they used to do it (the ring announcer at ringside instead of wrestlers marching down to the ring) and it's more realistic.

Watch the 'big' promoters and learn from their mistakes.

Chapter Ten

TEN QUESTIONS FOR PROMOTER MIKE MODEST

Mike Modest is not only a well respected wrestler but he is also a promoter for Pro Wrestling Iron (www.prowrestlingiron.com). We recently had the opportunity to ask about his perspective on promotions.

1. **How did you get involved with promoting professional wrestling?**

    My business partner, Donovan Morgan, and I are currently wrestlers for NOAH in Japan and we wanted to establish a place that was run by wrestlers not carneys or shady characters.

2. **Who is your favorite wrestler in PWI?**

    From a personal stand point myself. I am the greatest. From a business stand point probably Bison Smith because he is the strongest that we have now. He is an animal and does everything that he needs to do to achieve his goals.

3. **What is the hardest part of your job?**

    As a wrestler, it is the travel and as a promoter, it is advertising. Knowing where to advertise, how much to spend, what will be most sufficient. This is difficult.

4. **What advice would you give someone interested in being a promoter?**

    Be sure you know what you are getting yourself into. Know that you will lose money more than likely for quite awhile until your promotion gets out there and people get interested. Too many promoters think," Well, I will just bring in a bunch of name guys and then I will sell out." People still have to know about it in order to draw.

5. **What is the best part of your job?**
    Seeing a young wrestler get a break. I was there. I needed a break and got one when I needed it.

6. **What makes PWI unique from other promotions?**
    We are centered around wrestling and not silly gimmicks and story lines. We try to be more serious and treat this business with respect. All of our wrestlers know the basics of amateur wrestling. We are athletes.

7. **Where do you see the PWI in the future?**
    The future is hard to predict.

8. **If you have or had a son who wanted to get involved with wrestling, what would be your advice?**
    Finish school first so you have something to fall back on.

9. **Does the athletic commission affect you and to what capacity?**
    They try to bully wrestling promotions still. The athletic commission would have been an asset to wrestling had they taken it seriously but they wanted money for nothing. They did nothing to protect wrestlers, fans, or anyone else that matter except they helped themselves to promoter's money for years and put it all toward boxing. Wrestling got nothing in return for kicking 10% or 2000$ whatever is greater to the California Athletic commission. Basically, the California athletic commission acted like an organized crime syndicate collecting protection money.

10. **Does the strength or weakness of the WWE affect Indy wrestling, in your opinion?**
    WWE is both a good thing and bad thing for indy wrestling. They brought it into the mainstream. However, they have at the same time brainwashed fans to believe that gimmick and production are all that matter and that wrestling plays a small part in the overall product. They also market so well, kids don't want to see a local wrestler they only want to see the ROCK.

TEN QUESTIONS FOR A WRESTLING FAN

Jeffrey McCoy could be described as the typical fan. A husband and father of four, Jeffrey has been a long time professional wrestling observer. He resides in Northern California and is a manager for Xerox Corporation. These questions are aimed at providing the reader with another perspective.

1. **From a fan's perspective, what about the WWE keeps your interest?**

   The main factor that keeps me interested in the WWE is the athleticism of the wrestlers and the story lines. My wife likes to joke with me that wrestling is soap operas for men. It also does not hurt that the WWE is now the only major player in the market that provides this type of entertainment on a global scale.

2. **If you heard about an indy promotion moving into your area, what would cause you to go to one of their events (i.e. price, who was on the card, etc)?**

   The three main factors that would influence my decision to attend would be which wrestlers are on the card, ticket price, and venue. Name recognition and persona of the wrestler would have a definite impact on whether or not I would attend. The pricing would need to be substantially lower than attending a WWE event since an indy promotion is the equivalent of the minor leagues. And last, the venue would need to be accommodating with the necessary amenities (i.e.. snack bar, restrooms, security).

3. **If given the opportunity, how often would you go to see a wrestling event (i.e. once a month, twice a month) ?**

Probably once a month if the opportunity was available and the pricing was cost effective. Any event of this nature, or a sporting event that matter is much more electric and enjoyable LIVE.

4. What could a wrestling promotion do (if anything) that would make you uninterested in their product?

Going over the top with the sexual innuendos and the very low brow story lines. Wrestling fans may be predominately male blue collar working class, but they are not stupid and do not want to be entertained in a classless manner.

5. What would you like to see more of—more wrestling or more storylines ?

This form of entertainment is first about the athleticism and ability of the wrestlers. I would like to see more wrestling action and have the storylines be more secondary in support of the action. At times now, the

WWE is becoming more like MTV or ESPN. MTV and ESPN are supposed to be channels dedicated to music videos and sports reporting. However, both channels now provide very little of this type of entertainment and you need to watch their spin off channels to get your fix of music videos and sports reporting.

6. Do you watch Raw and/or Smackdown consistently?

I try to watch WWE Raw and Smackdown on a regular basis. I probably watch Smackdown more consistently since it comes at 8:00 PM and my kids are going to bed at this time. Raw is sometimes hard to watch consistently since it comes on at 6:00 pm on the West Coast and this is the time my family is eating dinner.

7. If an independent promotion were able to show their program on local television, would their lack of production capabilities deter you from enjoying their product ?

Not at all. As a spectator, you need to have a realistic expectation of what type of event you are watching. Similar to a sporting event, you would not expect the same atmosphere and product watching the San Jose Giants (minor league team) as you would watching the San Francisco Giants at Pacific Bell Park.

8. **Which advertising for a live event would get the most attention from you- television, radio, flier?**

Television would be the best medium to reach me and catch attention about an upcoming event. A direct e-mail campaign would also be effective with me since I do spend quite a bit of my spare time surfing the net.

9. **What could an indy promotion do, if anything, to get the majority of fans to pay attention?**

Provide a quality product and spread the word. If you provide customers with what they want, they will buy your product. But, you need to understand your customer's desires and expectations. Also, you need to get some exposure by promoting your product anywhere and everywhere that people will listen. Shameless, but ethical promotion.

10. **Do you see more or less popularity for wrestling in the years to come with the fans? with you?**

I believe that wrestling is at a crossroads. Without the competition of WCW and ECW, Vince McMahon and the WWE are not challenged to try new things and improve their product. Competition brings out the best in all of us and does not allow us to sit on our laurels and become complacent. They also need to cultivate new fans and continue to connect with the current fan base that is already established. The WWE seems to have gotten away from promoting and maintaining their product in a manner that made wrestling so popular in the 90's. My level of interest with wrestling will most likely slightly increase in the years to come as my children become older and more interested in this form of escapism entertainment.

Conclusion

A final word from the Equalizer -

We all have 'dreams' of what we are and what we'd like to become in life. Without a dream, you have no hope or no vision of where those roads are that lead to your dream.

No matter what, whether it be a wrestler, promoter, actor, businessman, or anything that you have the desire to do in life, always stay focused on that goal. Yes, you may have to do some jobs that you don't like, in order to pay the bills, but if you keep that goal in mind, eventually you will find that road and take it to your dream.

You don't want to look back years from now and think about the 'road not taken'. That could've been the one you wanted.

The Equalizer's Appendix
(Surgically Re-attached)

My Wrestling School
Complete Course $3000
10% discount (paid in full)
Includes First Pro Wrestling Match
(must be paid in full before able to wrestle first match)
Payments –OK $250 pr month or $45.00 pr session
Train 2 to 3 workouts per week.
Separate Ring workouts (uninstructed) $20 per person per hr.
Ring Rental $550 pr day.
Contract for payments school and ins. Waiver.

Wrestling Holds and Moves

Backdrop

Arm Drag
Tiltawhirl
Huricanrana
Slam
Powerbomb—
Sunset Flip

Monkey Flip

Frankensteiner
Flying HeadScissors
Kip up
Snap Mare
Bombs Away
Atomic Drop off of Headlock
Submission Arm Bar
Submission Bow and Arrow

Submission Camel clutch

Abdominal Stretch to Hip Toss
Hammer Lock
Head Lock

Wrist Lock

Dandido (pin)
Small Package
Back Slide
Hip Toss reverse
Stepover toe hold
Punches

Side Backdrop into an Arm drag
Japenese Arm drag
—Into a Slam or Backbreaker
Beal
Power Slam
False PowerBomb
Off the Ropes—out of the Corner
Off the ropes—out of the corner
Head Scissors

Chop Series
Full Nelson into a Snap Mare
From FullNelson
From Body Scissors
Submission Front Face Lock
Submission Hammerlock Choke
Submission Abdominal Stretch

Top Wrist Lock
Go Behind Take down—sit out into armdrag
Figure 4 leg lock—Inverted figure 4
School Boy
Headlock takeover
Hip Toss
Bulldog
Forearm smash (2 types)
Kicks (instep) Knee lifts

Back Kicks
Head into Turnbuckle
Backwards over Ropes
Taking bump over ropes
Back Rollups
Drop Kick
Leap Frog both ways
Leg Drag
(high spot)
knee, Jap arm drag

Head Butt
Test of strength
Coming over ropes front
First and Second Rope
Rollups off the ropes
Baseball Slide
Drop toe hold
Victory Roll
Head lock, tackle, down one

WRESTLING BUDGET

12 Wrestler @ $100 each—	$1200.00
1 Ring Rental $400	400.00
Timekeeper -	(usually find some to do
it for free)	
Announcer	(same)(Maybe A celebrity)
Referee- $100 (2)	$200.00
(someone in dressing room to get	
wrestlers in and out for the match)	volunteer
Ticket Takers	(undetermined)
Coordinating talent, show, set up	
(Ric)	(Fee to be discussed with
Topper)	
APPROXIMATE TOTAL	$2000.00

When I do an AWF Show, I usually get $2500.00 up front which covers most of my expenses and then do a % split at the gate.

Other expenses and conditions

Stage
Lighting
Sound
Chairs
Bleachers
Music
Dressing Area
Programs
Tickets
Advance Ticket sales
Smoke Machine for atmosphere

The Equalizer's Ten Steps to Promoting

1. Observe the competition (see what they are doing right and what they are doing wrong).
2. Seek ways to run shows inexpensively (I recommend fundraisers).
3. Brainstorm (take time to create a plan).
4. Set up a timeline (get your business license, insurance, and obligations to the athletic commission in order with plenty of time to promote your show—which should be a minimum of 3 to 4 months).
5. Seek out wrestlers.
6. Create a strategy for advertising (find your audience and give them a flier or two! Advertise on the internet).
7. Sign up volunteers (if this is a fundraiser, you are all set. With high schools, the sports team can serve as ticket takers, security and sell tickets before the show).
8. Plan for emergencies (make sure you have enough money before the show- too many promoters depend on the profits and then, when they don't come in, they stiff the wrestlers).
9. Give your audience what they want to see (if this is a high school, then keep the show clean so that you will be asked to return).
10. Treat the wrestlers and the audience well and you will build lasting contacts/friendships.

   With the 9/11 tragedy and the war, there's a lot of concern about personal safety when you're out on the streets and in public. Not to mention the fact that crimes against innocent folks are always in the headlines. Self defense in close quarters is something everyone should know about. In one of my upcoming books I will describe how things on your 'person' can be used to defend yourself, such as a shoelace, credit card, ink pen, etc. But out of all of those items, one of the best things yet is a new defense item that I have come up with called The Security Kat. It actually is a KEY CHAIN, but designed to hold in your hand with two fingers and keep any attacker away from you. It's made of durable acrylic, and fashionable as well, but can really save your life when you call upon it to do its' job. You can see this cute little item at www.securitykat.com . Make sure you get one for every member of your family and hope they never have to use it.

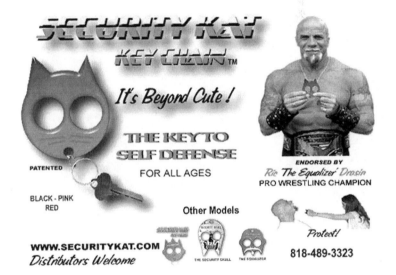

Watch out for those cheap shots in wrestling! Here, my son Shane, approaches me from behind as we shoot a great scene for a commercial.

It's always good to be the champ! Here I am with the American Wrestling Federation title belt (www.americanwrestlingfederation.com).

The American Wrestling Federation- the nicest and most professional bunch of wrestlers in North America.

No
Chicken Guts
for the
Wrestling Soul
REVISED

How to be a pro wrestling promoter like me
By Bruce Dwight Collins

Table of Contents

Introduction

1. My experience in wrestling
2. My company in print
3. You, the promoter vs. You, the owner
4. Opening Bell: The first things you should do
5. Preliminary Bouts: Getting organized, getting ready
6. Pinfalls and Submissions: Strength in Numbers
7. The Main Event: what your audience will experience?
8. Beyond Promoting: Expanding your opportunities
9. Time Limits: A few words about persistence
10. Closing Ring Announcements: Be a true champion

Welcome to

No Chicken Guts University

Introduction

Twelve minutes and thirty seconds of heart pounding, gut wrenching action. That's how long the two sweat soaked bruisers have been grappling in the ring. The fever pitch of the captivated audience rattles the sold out auditorium.

Boos stampede outward into the parking lot as the most hated wrestler they've ever loathed appears to be poised for victory. Just when any trace of hope seems to be dashed, the villain foolishly makes the classic mistake of turning his back on the fallen yet respected champion to taunt the frenzy fueled crowd.

This gives our hero the crucial time needed to recover and pin the repulsive wretch. A thunderous cheer rises to the building rafters as a noise competing ring bell clangs with piercing clarity. The ring announcer slips between the ropes and cries out that the champion has retained his title belt. An elated yet weary warrior stands victorious with heavyweight championship belt held high. The audience is captured in the moment.

The scores of fans exiting the night's festivities all leave with satisfied smiles on their faces and an impressive list of stories to tell in the days to come. Not only that, they can't wait to put down some hard earned cash when you bring back your wrestling company for the rematch.

Yes, YOU !

Wait, you're saying, I don't have the money to put together a wrestling show. I'll show you steps to make your shows affordable and profitable. Do wrestling companies go out of business ? Yes, they do but often it is the lack of common sense that dictates such a thing.

I think you can do it.

You might be thinking that you know nothing about promoting a show or owning a wrestling company. Perhaps you've dreamed of being a pro wrestling promoter but were overwhelmed with questions. You might also think that it takes years of being on the "inside" to run a successful wrestling operation.

Think again.

What you need more than anything else to succeed in any of life's precious goals is desire. Desire feeds your need for knowledge. That's why you are holding this book in your hand right now. You have the desire and you want the knowledge. Here it is, my friend.

This book will give you the tools to start your journey. Your desire will take you the rest of the way.

You might ask about the title. Why name it "No Chicken Guts for the Wrestling Soul" ? The only answer I have is that it seemed appropriate. Wrestling is not for the faint of heart. No matter what you hear from the average man or woman on the street, athletes in this sport pay a price. If you're not careful, you'll pay a price, too. So, take the tools that are offered in this book, apply them to your common sense and create within you an unstoppable force.

The title is also a spoof on the popular Chicken Soup books. I guess this is my version of wrestling self help. I have received a lot of compliments on the first edition. I hope you enjoy this revised copy, coupled with The Equalizer's writing.

This is not a book of guarantees but a vision of possibilities. As the saying goes, failure is the halfway point on the road to success. Perseverance is the vehicle to take you there.

Welcome to the life of a pro wrestling promoter. Enjoy the show !

Chapter 1

My Experience in Wrestling

Watching wrestling as a child, I never imagined that I would promote shows years later.

My grandfather, who was a preacher for over fifty years, was the other fan in the family. On Saturdays, I would arrive at my grandparents home early so that my grandfather and I could get together to watch our favorite hour. The program originated from a television studio in San Francisco and the poorly produced show attracted two rows of live audience.

Since we lived in the Bay Area, this was the wrestling that we knew. There were no nationwide wrestling companies but rather, territories. San Francisco's promoter was Roy Shires, whose promotion had membership in the National Wrestling Alliance or NWA. No other promotion dared to move into the Bay Area, it was sort of an unwritten wrestling code of honor. Despite the looks of the television show, the promotion was extremely popular and it was a frequent event for them to sell out the famous Cow Palace in San Francisco with a live card. The regulars were Pat Patterson, Ray Stevens, Dean Ho, Rocky Johnson, Pepper Gomez and Kenji Shibuya with an occasional appearance from the late Andre the Giant.

Back then, roller derby was on tv just before wrestling so we were treated to two hours of mayhem. I wanted to go to a live card at that time but since my father was not a wrestling fan, there was no possibility of that happening.

This shared love of wrestling was temporarily halted when my immediate family moved away from the Bay Area (and my grandparents) to Tucson, Arizona. I was disappointed in the fact that there were no local promotions on tv in Tucson. Not until Fritz Von Erich brought his 75 wrestling sons and his World Class Championship Wrestling to a new Catholic owned television station on the UHF dial. Believe it or not, they were the first station on the UHF dial in Tucson. It was a big deal. In case you are checking your pro wrestling reference manual, Fritz didn't actually have 75 sons but World Class had David, Kerry, Kevin, Mike, and Chris. What a tragic story in wrestling that was.

During the eight years of living in the cactus state and being away from the Clair Boreman-Bruce Collins weekly summits, the landscape of professional wrestling was slowly but gradually changing. Those promotions that had survived had wisely made themselves available to cable television. The WWF, the quickest at the starting line, was already beginning to rise in prominence even before the coronation of Hulk Hogan.

When I moved back to San Jose, California two months after high school graduation (also known as the 'big move of '86'), the tag team of Boreman and Collins resumed their couch warming Saturday ritual which now consisted of the WWF on WOR TV in New York, Georgia Championship Wrestling on Superstation TBS, and Fritz Von Erich's World Class somewhere on the tube.

By then, the World Wrestling Federation was rolling in the dough and rolling over the competition with it's huge closed circuit entertainment extravaganza known as WrestleMania.

The stars of wrestling and Hollywood were shining so bright that you could have been inspired to write a poem : Hulk Hogan, Mr. T, Liberace, Mohammed Ali. They were the wrestling pushers and I was hooked. My grandfather, who at this time was a retired minister, left church early to take me downtown to watch the first WrestleMania broadcast. In my mind, the highlight was when Andre the Giant lifted 6'10" Big John Studd over his head for an unbelievable bodyslam.

Studd and Bobby "the Brain" Heenan had fanned the flames by offering $10,000 to anyone who could bodyslam Studd in the months prior to WrestleMania. They had successfully averted parting with the cash and thereby, created a huge build up prior to the match.

I remained a loyal fan into the early 90's but unfortunately, my grandfather passed away in February of 1990. He was 81 years old. My grandfather was a good person and the decisions he made early in his life (particularly the spiritual ones) influenced his offspring. In regards to wrestling, I'm not sure I became a fan because of him but when I now look back with a certain sense of nostalgia, the memories are as much of my grandfather as they are of Pat Patterson or Ray Stevens. My thoughts revolve less around the specifics of a cage match in 1981 as my grandfather yelling at the referees because they didn't see a tag team double teaming some poor guy (he was pretty adamant that wrestling was not fake and back then, not one wrestler would have said it was). I know that I will never have a wrestling 'kindred spirit' to the degree that my grandfather and I shared. Although my brother Brent and his wife Liz are wrestling fans, when I would get together with my grandfather on Saturdays, wrestling was a huge part of our dialogue. Wrestling will never be the same since he passed away.

For several years after my grandfather's death, I slowly lost interest in wrestling. I gave up on WrestleMania when the WWF announced that football great Laurence Taylor, who had never stepped into a wrestling ring, and Bam Bam Bigelow were going to face each other in the main event of the most prestigious wrestling pay per view of 1995.

My favorite wrestler was, is and will be Jake "The Snake" Roberts. Jake has always been the standard in pro wrestling, as far as I'm concerned. What I mean by that is, Jake had all the tools necessary to make a great wrestler. He had great ring presence in addition to an unparalleled gift of giving the best promos (interviews) in professional wrestling. His skills were so refined that he could be the most beloved face on Sunday and the most vile heel on Monday. I could say more but I'm guessing that you know I'm a huge Jake Roberts fan.

So, for a few years in the mid-nineties, I was not indulging myself in the WWF's 'new generation'. Apparently, neither were many of you. The WWF's fanbase dropped considerably during those years and WCW, under Mr. Turner, began to build an empire in Atlanta. A large portion of WWF talent with names like Hogan, Savage, Nash, Hall, Piper, DiBiase, Luger, and finally Hart, migrated south for a very long Federation winter.

My interest in the 'squared circle' was resurrected by the resurgence of the WWF in 1998. Ted Turner's WCW was cash plenty and talent deep and forced the struggling Federation into a new concept, WWF attitude. Well, forced might be a strong word but I suppose that they felt they had to abandon all the things that had worked in the past because they weren't working at that moment. The attitude brought a more adult oriented program to television.

Although WCW had a healthy supply of talent, their use of these superstars and the storylines that were weaved around them were often a seemingly misguided pile of nonsense. If the stories were weaved, the garment wouldn't have passed thrift store standards. Often, feuds were not explained acceptably, champions were crowned predictably and sometimes ideas were abandoned midway into the plot. For a company that had a mountain high roster of veterans, their pay per views were often a molehill of 25% undercard athletes. Every single pay per view could have been the equivalent of a wrestling all star game but they chose Fit Finlay and Disco Inferno instead. Meanwhile, the WWF's shocking, sensationalistic shows were making all the noise. On Monday nights, you were given the choice of watching a G rated wrestling show that made no sense or a PG-13 rated program that was also engaging with or without the adult slant. By the way, I'm not condoning the WWF's decision as you'll read later.

It didn't take long for the competition, which was drawing new fans every week in the ratings, to help the rise of a third wrestling company, Extreme Championship Wrestling or ECW. ECW benefited from the hype that was being generated by the 'main event', McMahon vs. Turner. Extreme was just that. ECW was the radical bloody, violent and sexually explicit version of mainstream wrestling. Paul Heyman, who was once manager Paul E. Dangerously in WCW, was the owner of this up and coming organization. At the height of their popularity, ECW was on tv in markets across the United States, offering pay per views, toys and a monthly magazine. Their big break came when they landed a national show on cable tv's TNN network on Friday nights.

In early 1998, my brother directed my attention to a now defunct website, Goplay.com, which offered free email and website hosting services. I thought it would be fun to experiment on a webpage but had to think a little while on what I wanted the site to be about. Finally, it came to me like a bolt of lightning or a steel chair to the head. The WCW Haters Club was formed that day. I wasn't a fan of everything that McMahon did. He had his own share of detractors yet I was even more troubled by Ted Turner's attempt to control wrestling with his wallet. Looking back, it's sort of funny that there was a fear of a WCW monopoly when the course of time has shown it's the other way around. Most fans that I met during this time were also bothered that Turner didn't appear to be interested in the wrestling portion of the business but rather, the business portion of the wrestling. That became painfully obvious as time passed. Candidly, I also wasn't a big fan of Turner's ultra-liberal political views.

My webpage brought together scores of wrestling fans from around the globe. On the suggestion of a WCW Haters frequent visitor, I started selling two wrestling parody t-shirts. The first shirt boldly proclaimed "WCW Haters Club" at the top with a cartoonish likeness of Austin, Undertaker and Kane manhandling a likeness of Turner. Austin was pulling on his tie if I remember right. The second shirt stated "Goldberg Sucks !" and featured a detailed drawing of Goldberg as an infant, complete with pacifier, diaper and Hollywood Hogan doll. This was a statement on WCW's push (or promotion) of a relative rookie in wrestling. Basically, he was the WCW's answer for the popularity of Steve Austin. I'm not taking anything away from Goldberg, either. He was enormously popular in 1998.

Interest in the club peaked between late '98 and early '99. We had daily columnists, chats and email campaigns. We were on all of the major search engines so anyone with a grudge toward WCW could easily access us. Despite the growing number of visitors to the site, it's doubtful that we ever made much of an impact upon the ratings or revenue of either company but at least we had found a shared virtual community where we could vent.

During the height of my webpage's popularity, the t-shirts were selling faster than a flying forearm. This was a shock to me initially. Never had I achieved monetary success in any previous entrepreneurial venture. The positive reaction to these unique shirts was overwhelmingly reaffirming so I reasoned that I was doing something right. I decided to expand my method of sales and received even more orders. My investment of $5 per shirt was paid back to me when half of the shirts were sold. Online auctions seemed to reap the best sales for me. I once sold a shirt for $47 on Ebay. Expecting a disappointed reaction from the buyer, I felt so bad I sent the customer an additional shirt but he was thrilled upon receipt of the merchandise. The shirts were meant to be advertising for the WCW Haters but I never dreamed that they would supplement my income.

At around this time, I received an email from Mark Anderson. Anderson was in his early twenties and after viewing my website, was interested in linking his page to mine and vice versa. By adding a link to each other's webpage, we would hopefully increase the number of hits (or visits) to our sites.

Mark's internet page was fairly new but he had a great idea- an audio wrestling show. You could download the show on Monday nights before WWF's Raw on USA or WCW's Nitro on TNT. The show usually lasted an hour and featured opinions, news and rumors but the highlight every week was the interviews with wrestling superstars such as Jake "The

Snake" Roberts, the Honky Tonk Man, or Dan "The Beast" Severn , who was not only a wrestler but a former Ultimate Fighting Champion.

I'm not convinced that linking our pages brought more visitors to our sites but I am convinced that this chance encounter with someone thousands of miles away in Eastern Canada changed my life. The internet, email and technology in general has allowed common folks like myself to make connections with people I'd never have the opportunity of meeting otherwise.

Several months later, I sent Mark an email asking him how his webpage was going. He replied that things were going great although his show's co-host, who I only knew as 'Temporary Insanity', was leaving to go to college. Then at the bottom of his email he nonchalantly mentioned that he was expanding his site to include a wrestling organization, the Hardcore Wrestling Federation. He felt that he had enough contacts and resources within the industry to create a new promotion in the Toronto area.

In April of 1999, the Hardcore Wrestling Federation had a robust debut with its' first show, Meltdown '99. Mark's company had all the hardcore style matches you could ask for, including: weapons matches, ladder matches, matches with thumbtacks, tables on fire, first blood matches, and anything else that was appropriate to the name Hardcore. The show was a financial success and Hardcore was in business. Before long, I saw the name HWF make the rounds on all the popular wrestling internet rumor sites.

I'm not going to tell you that I had anything to do with Mark's business, because I didn't. The only thing I was able to do was contribute to some of the writing on his webpage. I decided not only to write the news but I felt like I could develop some interest in Hardcore by creating the news. For instance, Hardcore was employing former WWF wrestler, Bastion Booger. Since Jesse Ventura, a former wrestler, was hot in the media with his political victory in Minnesota, I came up with an idea revolving around Governor Ventura. Jesse had stated in one of his speeches that he was trading in his wrestling nickname of "The Body" for a new one, "The Mind". I wrote a front page article that Bastion was appointing himself as the new "Body". If you've ever seen Bastion "The Body" Booger, you know he's not an ounce over 350 pounds. Booger's new contradictory nickname got a lot of attention on the internet. Steve Lombardi, who was booked for the show as the Brooklyn Brawler and Doink the Clown at Meltdown '99, had a good laugh with Mark over the story.

Another story I wrote was a so-called rumor that the Brooklyn Brawler was training in Harlem with former WWF star Bad News Brown. Bad News, who once brought a caged rat to ringside in a match against Jake Roberts at a WWF SummerSlam pay per view, was showing the Brawler how to be tough by giving him a lesson in Bad News cuisine. Brown was getting Brooklyn ready by dining him on those famous Harlem rats. Of course, I made the whole rodent tale (or tail) up. I haven't a clue where Bad News is today but it made for an eye catching, if not stomach turning, literary masterpiece worthy of tabloid publication.

As Hardcore began to do monthly shows, I thought about the possibility of running shows in California. The choice on one hand was exhilarating and on the other hand intimidating. After much thought, I decided that if I was ever going to give it a try, now was the time. I told Mark about my intentions and that I would do my best to bring his champion, Tommy Twilight, to San Jose. By this time, Hardcore Wrestling was getting a lot of press in Canada. Anderson had told me that Paul Heyman of ECW had personally called him to become Extreme's Canadian promoter as ECW wanted to make inroads north of their operations. The owner of ECW was asking a 23 year old man with no previous experience to take over his promotions in Canada ! Heyman gave him one condition to his offer, Mark would have to fold up his own wrestling tent. My friend declined. We had decided that if we were going to be in this business it would have to be because we loved doing it.

That meant personal enjoyment and creative freedom carried a heavier weight than profit margin.

Meanwhile, I had attended some local indy shows to view the competition. In the Bay Area, All Pro Wrestling was the indy powerhouse at the time. They were running mostly fundraisers and generally drew 400 people per show in high school gymnasiums. The Silicon Valley area is one of the toughest places to run a wrestling show. There are so many avenues of spectator fun fighting for everyone's disposable entertainment buck. Yet, APW was doing quite well with attendance figures. Big Time Wrestling was also operating in Northern California but with less professionalism and a much smaller audience. Their promoter/owner was too focused on his 'cash cow' autograph sessions. His shows were not only out of focus, you could have developed a better plot yourself looking at them with a glass eye. The natural progression of a wrestling event just wasn't there.

Two of APW's superstars, Mike Modest and Donovan Morgan, were head and shoulders above any other indy wrestlers in technique and skill. I was also impressed by a tag team from Southern California, the Ballard Brothers. The Ballards ,who are identical twins, are a high flying combo and make for a great tag team. They dress in hockey uniforms and are reminiscent of the Hanson brothers in the Paul Newman movie, Slapshot.

An acquaintance was also made with actor, wrestler, wrestling school trainer/owner, and promoter, Ric "the Equalizer" Drasin. Ric's credentials are impressive and he's someone with a lot of integrity. He designed the Gold's Gym logo and was an early training partner of Arnold Schwarzeneggar. He had a regular job as one of the 'transforming' Hulks (who appear before the complete change to Lou Ferrigno) in the Incredible Hulk tv show, and has appeared in numerous movies and television commercials. He's also wrestled all over the country and was originally trained by Mae Young, legendary female wrestler. Ric was one of the early "bodybuilder" type wrestlers who ushered in a more "in shape" look to grapplers in North America.

While my list of contacts were building, my reliance on the two local promotions, All Pro Wrestling and Big Time Wrestling, was causing me a forehead full of headaches. In a business environment such as wrestling, I've learned that the less dependent you need to be on others, the better. Compare it to a feeding frenzy at Sea World and you're the new whale in the tank. Doubtful that the toothy killers would drop the bloody flesh hanging out of their mouths to give you some gentle advice on using a fork and knife. Don't be surprised if they look at you like you are their next meal. Yet, I was naïve and new to the ring of pond scum that was Bay Area wrestling.

Many wrestling promoters steep themselves in arrogance. They feel you have to be an insider in wrestling to succeed. They think you had to wrestle at some point or at least that you were once a snot nosed kid who rang the bell for free. This isn't the case but the more you believe them, the less you will believe in yourself.

Due to the growing mistrust I had toward local promotions, I brought several indy wrestlers from the Los Angeles area to my show. I'm glad that I did. The Ballard Brothers, Big Schwag, the Hardcore Kid, and Mike Henderson were not only great mat artists but they were also very nice people which helps to make things smoother the day of the event. All of them exhibited a very professional attitude.

I had decided to run my first show in October and I called it Halloween Horror '99. I also decided to name my wrestling operation, Boreman's Wrestling Planet. I figured that if you want to stand out, you start with your name. I wanted to generate interest in a relatively unknown product. Boreman was my grandfather's last name and I wanted the BWP to reflect his values. You could say that his values were reminiscent of an earlier time in wrestling. No profanity, excessive violence or adult content. I wanted to appeal to the families who felt that wrestling was turning its' back on them. I also wanted to be proud of it myself, which is one of the reasons why I could not work for the other two promotions. If I can't be proud of it then it wouldn't be worth the effort. Nothing makes me more uneasy than people acting irresponsibly around impressionable children.

During the summer months of 1999, I juggled a job with Xerox and another more fascinating vocation. There were a lot of things to plow through including the preparation of the advertising of the event. Ric "the Equalizer" Drasin was very helpful in this area. First, he designed a poster with a creepy haunted house on it and listed some of the wrestlers who would be at the event: Honky Tonk Man, Doink the Clown, Ric Drasin,

Big Schwag, Mike Modest, Maxx Justice, Donovan Morgan, the Ballard Brothers, Suicide Kid, Freddie Valentine and Shane '54. Then, Ric allowed me to use some footage for my commercial which was from a very popular Redman/ Method Man rap video "Tear It Off" that Ric and some of his wrestlers were in. The video had a wrestling theme and my commercial showed a sold out audience engaged in a lively match. The icing on the cake was that the referee in the commercial was the actor who played Mini Me in the Austin Powers movies.

Leading up to the event, I made a lot of contacts in the Bay Area which included television and radio personalities, promoters, venue representatives, and fans. Best of all, I was able to communicate with many legendary wrestlers who I had watched as a youngster. My favorite moments were when King Kong Bundy called me back and admonished me for leaving more than one message on his answering machine. Another time I offended Afa from the 70's/ 80's tag team, the Wild Samoans, because I kept asking him questions thru email and never did business with him. Friendship is rarely offered in this business but often is sold for questionable rates.

I was in touch with several radio stations around San Jose and booked some time on the San Jose State University morning show. The University is only a few blocks from the Civic Auditorium. My thought was that I was hitting my target audience. The three wrestlers who I had booked to be on the show were Mike Modest, the Honky Tonk Man and Ric Drasin. Unfortunately, Modest was unable to reach me in time to work out the details. So, in rare wrestling form, I placed the microphone in front of me and, totally unscripted, communicated my views on the state of wrestling for a solid hour. I had my mom tape the entire show but sadly, the entire broadcast was eaten up by a faulty cassette player.

Unsure of how the event would sell on "game day", I bulked up the event with low paid talent. A friend of mine named Efrem White was helping me with the show. He offered the services of his brother who owned an independent music label called Undercover Records. Eric White's rap artist, M. C. Dee, was booked as additional entertainment. I can't tell you how much help the White brothers were that day.

The San Jose Civic Auditorium opened its' doors at 6:30 pm on October 15, 1999. All the sweat and undue stress from other promoters came to a halt and "Halloween Horror" took control of the situation.

Two and a half hours of bodyslams and dropkicks.

It didn't stop after the event was over, either. My event was critiqued, ridiculed, and complimented on the internet, in articles and among rival promoters. All I had to do was put the phrase "Halloween Horror" into a search engine and article after article appeared from various wrestling webpage sources.

Boreman's Wrestling Planet had arrived and the idea was birthed that anyone could promote if they wanted to take the chance. It was possible. The insiders had to move over in the pew and allow some room for another soul.

"Halloween Horror '99" and the subsequent events since then are discussed later in the book. As you'll see, this business is never dull but it is definitely yours if you so choose.

Chapter 2

My Company in print

Free publicity is a beautiful thing. Wrestling legend and current employee of World Wrestling Entertainment, Pat Patterson, was once quoted as saying "all publicity is good publicity". In a sense, I suppose that's true unless you're the type of person to care about your reputation. If you want to have a sense of integrity attached to your name (which strangely is a rare desire in wrestling), you had better make sure you conduct your business honestly. I always believe you reap what you sow and bad publicity will come back to haunt you.

After the smoke had settled from my event, more controversy in local wrestling followed. Particularly interesting was one event held by Big Time Wrestling. One of the performers at the 'Big Time' event confronted APW's owner, Roland Alexander. SF Weekly, a free entertainment magazine in the Bay Area, dispatched a reporter, Mark Athitakis, to sort out the situation. He reported:

'Then the Blue Meanie suddenly climbed out of the ring and stalked across the running track toward the stands. The spectators may have assumed this was all part of the wrestling script, but in fact it was very real. The Blue Meanie stopped and pointed toward one of the bleachers, which was nearly empty except for a fat man calmly eating nachos next to his girlfriend. Jasmin St. Clair couldn't show her face tonight, the Blue Meanie exclaimed, because of that man: Roland Alexander, the bitter rival promoter, the jerk...Alexander got St. Clair pulled from the show, the Blue Meanie said, by calling the school and telling the administration a porn star was going to perform.

Alexander himself sat impassively and said nothing. His girlfriend stood up to protest, only to be quickly dispatched as "trailer trash." As the Blue Meanie was coaxed back into the ring, a befuddled audience was left wondering what had just happened.

The match went on, but it was hardly the end of the matter. For weeks afterward, Internet message boards, pro wrestling magazines, and wrestlers themselves couldn't escape the topic. The event's promoter, Kirk White, had his suspicions—Roland Alexander had screwed with his operation before, and it seemed like just the sort of stunt he'd pull. Jasmin St. Clair summed things up on her Web site, where she offered fans her opinion of Alexander: "Some local indie jamboni had me thrown off the show out of jealousy," she wrote, "since he never has any big names on his show, has talentless boys, and a Bob's Big Boy-looking white trash girlfriend that stenches up any room she walks into."

As it happens, nobody called the school to try to ruin its fund-raiser. The high school's administrators had noticed the ads for the event, which prominently featured the scantily clad St. Clair, and asked Kirk White to cancel her appearance. But the fact that so many people believed Roland Alexander could have done it speaks volumes about the level of bitterness, suspicion, and cutthroat behavior that suffuses local independent wrestling promotions. It's a war in which events are allegedly sabotaged, rivals are bad-mouthed on the Internet, and wrestlers are treated like indentured servants.

As wars go, the stakes are petty: The reward is

success in a small and only modestly profitable world. Nevertheless, independent promotions here and across the country have bloomed again in the last three years, riding the coattails of the massive success of the World Wrestling Federation. They lack the style and pyrotechnics of the big-name events clogging prime-time cable TV, but they keep hard-core fans sated when TV matches aren't enough and six months is too long to wait for the next live event.

In the Bay Area, everybody agrees that trying to do shows in big cities is usually a waste of time—the sophisticated residents of San Francisco, Oakland, San Jose, and Berkeley won't sully their hands with something so gauche as wrestling—so most matches are staged in the Bay Area's outer rim of bedroom communities: Healdsburg, Galt, Antioch, Union City, and Vallejo. Matches are broadcast on public access channels in Newark, Fremont, Foster City, and elsewhere. The matches themselves are held at high schools and Boys Clubs; because they're often fund-raisers, profits are slim.

In such a market, getting your piece in the Bay Area means playing a bit of hardball. In fact, sometimes it seems promoters have learned to run their companies by watching what happens in a ring.

Today, three promoters work the Bay Area: Roland Alexander of All Pro Wrestling, Kirk White of Big Time Wrestling, and Bruce Collins of upstart Boreman's Wrestling Planet. To varying degrees, each feels burned by the other two, either by actual actions or perceived slights. Observers, including the wrestlers themselves, wish it could be otherwise. But the egos are too strong and the skins are too thin.'

As you can see, it pays to work on your reputation. Of course, the article covered the seedy history of the BTW (Kirk White)/APW (Roland Alexander) feud so I was sent to the end of the story. This was probably a good thing because it didn't seem to be particularly flattering toward White and Alexander. The author, Mark Athitakis, seemed like a nice guy who wanted to make sure he had his facts straight and touched base with me many times after the initial interview. I was extremely happy with the write up and made dozens of copies to disperse. Here was my early fifteen minutes of journalistic fame:

'Bruce Collins, the Bay Area's other promoter, was blind to all this squabbling when he started his company last year, but it didn't take him long to get embroiled in it. He is a man apart from the White and Alexander model of a promoter—proud, noisy, and *this close* to getting really pissed off. Collins, by contrast, is a techie by trade, bespectacled and goateed; instead of talking like he has something to prove, he speaks gently. Pro wrestling was the one connection he had with his late grandfather, Clair Boreman. Collins got his start selling T-shirts parodying well-known wrestlers, and after building up a few contacts, he decided to start his own wrestling promotion. Boreman's Wrestling Planet, he called it, in honor of his grandfather, and he fashioned it in the style of wrestling his grandfather liked—the no-frills fundamentals with none of the explosions, foulmouthed bickering, and mature-audience content. "I wanted it to be something that everybody in the family could go see," he says. "Today, if you go to the indie shows, they're greatly affected by the WWF and WCW, so much so that now you have guys flipping off little kids in the audience, even when it's a smaller indie promotion."

Collins is wary about discussing what happened to his first event last Halloween—he fears a possible backlash that could prevent him from putting on another event. And while he admits he is new to the business, he doesn't think that excuses the way he was treated—which has left him with a lingering sense that his show was sabotaged. At first, Collins was using a couple of wrestlers from Southern California and had a few contacts there to help with logistics. But for cost-efficiency, he handled matters such as renting a ring and hiring other wrestlers locally. He put in calls to Roland Alexander and Kirk White.

White's first question to Collins was a pointed one: Was he going to use any of Alexander's wrestlers? Alexander's response, on the other hand, was, ""You're competing with me in my market, and for me to do that I would need some kind of percentage,'" says Collins. Eventually he reached agreements with both promoters: He would use two of Alexander's wrestlers—Morgan and Modest—but most of the other wrestlers, and the ring, would come from Big Time Wrestling.

"I have no complaints with the wrestlers themselves," Collins recalls. "Everybody was very professional." The problem, he says, came from Kirk White, who seemed to change the wrestlers he was offering daily. Collins also claims he got a call from the Elvis-themed Honky Tonk Man, one of the wrestlers flying in, saying he wasn't coming because Kirk White said the show was canceled. As a result, Collins felt that control of the show was falling out of his hands. "It was almost like there were stumbling blocks placed in my way, so that I couldn't concentrate on actually promoting the show," says Collins, who couldn't announce a bill if he didn't know who was on it.

"Halloween Horror '99" was supposed to be two events—one at the 2,000-seat San Jose Civic Auditorium, and another the following night at the Cactus Club, a San Jose nightclub. But with all the chaos, word didn't get out very well. Fewer than 200 people showed up for the first night. The second was canceled after his original venue fell through at the last minute. Which was probably just as well, since the ring Collins rented from White barely fit in the club anyway.

"I gave him half the money back [on the ring]," White says. "I bent over backward trying to give him suggestions. He lost his ass on his own."

Collins also managed to antagonize Alexander. "Yeah, I was upset that he didn't use my boys," Alexander says, although he believes Collins knows better now.

The new promoter has indeed learned a few lessons. Next time he'll rent a ring from out of town, Collins says, and use more out-of-town wrestlers, too. And if he has to use local talent, he'll go with APW alone and avoid getting in the middle of a turf war.

But the whole ugly experience has left him with a distaste for the business. "I'd kind of been under the impression that these promoters will do anything to stop you from getting any kind of publicity for your event," Collins says. "I think in many ways I injured the pride of both Kirk and Roland for using their competitor's respective wrestlers. I think the wounds between them are so deep, it was a bad idea to try to make a show work using wrestlers from two separate promotions. Big mistake."

True to form, Roland Alexander dismisses Collins' event in his patented style. "The wrestlers were not professional," he says. "This is a guy who knows nothing about wrestling other than what he's learned on the Internet."

But in a strange way he may also sympathize with Collins' new attitude toward the profession. "The industry can be one that you love, because it's been in your blood, but it's also a business of love-hate, because of the politics," Alexander says. "People say, 'There's politics everywhere. There was politics when you were an accountant.' Sure there were politics when I was an accountant. But not like this stuff.'"

Spoken like an expert.

Other parts of the article I enjoyed were a series of little blurbs where the vile hatred between White and Alexander began to volley back and forth in rhetorical comments and fuzzy accusations. Let the comedy begin!

- (Kirk) White says he would never attack the quality of All Pro Wrestling's operation. But he also doesn't mind sharing a few stories about wrestlers who have worked for Alexander and have claimed poor pay and lousy treatment.

- Alexander's venom extends to Big Time Wrestling's Kirk White as well: Sitting in his office a few days after the Blue Meanie incident, Alexander has a few choice words to say about the event's promoter. He spins a lively conspiracy theory about Jasmin St. Clair's non-appearance at the high school, a tangled web of late-night phone calls and undercover operations, but the upshot is his sense that Kirk White may have been trying to create controversy against him. "I'm not ruling out that he decided to use [St. Clair] in his advertising to see what he could draw from it, then decides to make up a story about people calling the school...and saying, "Roland is the guy who did it,'" he says. "I'm not ruling that out, because I know Kirk White is just a real piece of garbage."

Why would he do such a thing?

Alexander thinks for a moment.

"I think he's a sicko," he says. "I think he gets his kicks out of something like that."

- "The wrestling business is a cutthroat business as it is, and personally I don't think [Alexander] did it," he (Kirk White) says. Still, he admits that he first thought of Alexander when the high school officials started protesting. "When I got these phone calls [from the school], sure, Roland's name came to mind, just like if I did something to his show he'd probably think the same of me."

What, Kirk???

Finally, Ric Drasin wrote an article on his webpage (www.americanwrestlingfederation.com) regarding my show.

'I recently worked a show with my Son in San Jose for a promoter who's just getting started. It was his first show. His name is Bruce Collins and…a nice guy who looked to me for advice. I don't normally travel to do someone else's show but I could see he was lost and wanted to help. I sent him 7 of the Wrestlers that I use, including my son and myself to work the show. I guided him through the advertising process and the Do's and Don'ts of the business. He was very appreciative. The big problem that I found was he had two rivals up there, APW's Roland Alexander (which is mentioned in Barry Blaustein's 'Beyond the Mat' documentary) and Big Time Wrestling , owned by Kirk White. These two men did everything possible to completely wipe out his show. BTW rented him the ring, and then called the Athletic commission to close him down, told wrestlers not to show and on the 2nd night, said his ring wouldn't fit in the building and there wasn't enough room to walk by to the restroom. This was false but the show was cancelled anyway. APW showed up and created problems with the promoter because he didn't use his 'boys' and then wrote a terrible article (one man point of view) on the internet about the show.
The show was good.'

All this time, you thought all the action was in the ring. No, it's only now that you have embarked on the adventure of a lifetime. This is the world of wrestling promotions!

Chapter 3

You, the promoter vs. You, the owner

With every decision that you make in life, the end result probably has a series of positive and negative outcomes. For instance, losing weight may mean denying yourself the pleasure of a banana split. However, the rewarding outcome is a healthier body. Many times, you have to study the possibilities and decide if the advantages outweigh the disadvantages. Other times, you may simply go with a gut feeling or an overpowering desire to live out a dream or a goal despite the risk involved.

When starting out this dream, you will be involved in independent, more commonly known as indy, wrestling. When the WWF, WCW and ECW were the "Big 3", they were known as national promotions and their titles were known as World Titles. This was because they toured a large portion of the United States and had wrestling programs in syndication and also on cable television. All other companies were known as indy promotions because they were primarily regional. Today, all companies in the United States except for the WWE are indy. This is not to say that your options are limited. Eventually, you may get noticed by the WWE and promote for them or your company may rise to national distinction with some nice television deal. You may one day 'wrestle' with shareholders and your celebrity mug will be viewed at different angles in different magazines. All things are possible.

Deciding whether promoting or owning a wrestling

company is right for you may not be clear at the moment but a few tips will go a long way toward your decision. When you are equipped with knowledge, you have the direction necessary in defining your ambition.

First, let's look at the basic differences between a promoter and an owner. A promoter can be an owner and vice versa. However, they can also be mutually exclusive from each other. Both jobs are important to the success of any wrestling operation.

The promoter's basic responsibility is to promote. This means that the promoter organizes a specific wrestling show or series of shows. This is a time consuming task. He or she takes care of the advertising, ticket distribution, radio promotions, venue preparation, and many more aspects pertaining to the organizing of the event including the resolution of unforeseen problems. In short, the promoter does everything in his power to insure a smooth wrestling presentation and to maximize ticket sales or profits. This is done through a building repertoire of contacts, ideas, planning and skill.

Again, an owner can promote his company's matches but sometimes, for various reasons, he or she relies on promoters. An owner may not want to immerse themselves into the detailed task and necessary commitment to time that promotions insist of you. Instead, they may opt to focus on the daily business operation. This is especially true of a larger company or an owner who is busy with other ventures outside of wrestling.

While there is no clear cut answer as to which decision you should make, there are definite questions you should ask yourself. One question in particular might give you the ultimate answer immediately. First, how much responsibility do I want resting on my shoulders ?

The ownership role affords you maximum creative control but also burdens you with the maximum degree of risk. Remember, when I say burden that this is based on perspective. It's only a burden if the risk is going to ruin you financially. It's always best to start safely and slowly, increasing your knowledge every step of the way. A promoter's risk is usually on a 'per show' basis but many decisions won't be yours to make.

Let's suppose that your only interest is in promoting occasional cards. How do you start? Where do you start? This is where the homework begins. Remember, for everything you want to do in life, someone did it first.

Study the wrestling scene in your area. This is beneficial in multiple ways. Find out who the established wrestling companies are in your community. Avoid the backyard wrestling or even the hint of a federation being run like a backyard promotion. You are professional and you will be looking for professional companies. As you probably know, professional does not always mean reputable but it's a good place to start. Go to as many live wrestling events as you can to see what your potential fans' expectations are.

The biggest risk in promoting for a company with no ownership power of your own is that you are solely relying on the reputation of that owner. You have to be able to trust the person you are working for, which begs of you to do some research. Obviously, the more research you do now, the less dependence on aspirin later. Your best bet is to talk to promoters who are currently employed by the company. Better yet, try to find promoters who have left the organization. Granted, many of them will probably have slanted and disgruntled opinions but take time to see if there are any patterns that ring true (I'll let you decide if there was a pun intended). If you even have the slightest hint of something fishy, take your fishing pole elsewhere and stay away from that promotion. Many people make their greatest mistakes when they don't trust that nagging warning sign they feel inside.

Once you've established that the ownership has a good reputation, you need to find out what the typical arrangement is between the boss and his promoters. After all, establishing honesty doesn't guarantee a fair monetary relationship. It is possible to run across someone who won't lie to you but will display greedy tendencies. Several questions should be asked at this time and specific answers from those in charge should be expected by you. Those questions include: how much money am I expected to put up ? what type of support will I get from the wrestling company ? What percentage of the profit will I take home ? The answers need to satisfy you. Their answers should include: you only need to put up some of the money, you will be supported by us through as many promotional avenues as we can tap into (they need to support you somehow otherwise, what is the sense in working with them at all ?), and your percentage will be much greater than ours. Vague responses are not acceptable and it would even be a good idea to put everything on paper with accompanying signatures. If anything, this will be a pretty good indication to them that you will not be duped into doing something unreasonable.

Most owners need you more than you need them so remember, all of these aspects of the event are negotiable. On the business side, think of wrestling as the Tijuana gift shop of sports. Everything can be bargained and you are the one with the muscle. A local wrestling establishment would rather have you working with them than against them.

Another piece of advice I need to pass on is, think of wrestling as a card game with Jesse James. Never let an owner see what is up your sleeve until complete trust is attained. What happened to me in my experience was that I trusted a few owner/promoters too soon before I knew them and later, reaped the misfortune. If you find yourself looking to another owner or to taking on the responsibility of ownership yourself, you don't want 'loose lips' to bury you before you begin. Also, don't close the business deal too early. Time is on your side and the more information you acquire about your new amigos will go a long way toward your sanity.

If you feel unsure about your future plans in the sport, promoting for an owner will give you an easier way to exit wrestling if your first event cuts off the sails of your enthusiasm vessel.

However, you may have decided that wrestling ownership is your choice. For you, the benefits and creative control outweigh the risks. At least if you are the boss, you know that you can depend on yourself.

Either way, if you are serious about entering the world of pro wrestling, you will encounter setbacks. I wish I could say that is not the case. Yet, just like in a wrestling match, promoting often resembles a roller coaster ride. Do not be discouraged, you'll find that each step is a learning experience and eventually you will build a loyal fanbase.

If things are not going your way at the moment, the worst thing you can do is panic. I knew a promoter who wasn't doing very well promoting his company. Instead of taking a month or two off to regroup and assess his next move, he scheduled 3 shows in a row in cities near his hometown. In a moment of sheer lunacy on his part, he figured that going "all out" would help him land a great deal of money. This is the same mentality of a losing Vegas gambler (do any of them really win?). Needless to say, he could not devote his time to promoting three different shows and all of them suffered. When the weekend was over, he had lost over $10,000.

Ego is another setback which will adversely affect your pocketbook. One promoter on the West Coast decided to hold an indy tournament here as they do on the East Coast. East Coast indies typically do greater business than West Coast. They might do two or three shows a week, whereas West Coast companies are lucky to do one a month. It seemed like a personal vendetta to prove his eminence with East Coast promotions. He flew in Indy workers from all over the country (usually airfare is reserved for a "big name" wrestler who will draw an audience). The average wrestling fan has never heard of these guys and the company was rumored to have lost $12,000. All of this was done only because someone wanted to inflate their importance. Check your mental health at the door because wrestling is not a place to lose your astuteness.

There seems to be an unwritten rule in wrestling and among the internet critics that you are not a 'real' promotion unless you are regularly performing shows. This is ridiculous.

Don't be pressured to make unwise business decisions based on peer pressure.

That's what I like about Ric Drasin. He does shows when they are economically viable. He puts events together when there is a very good chance of making a profit. He isn't pressured to put together shows on anyone else's timetable. That's intelligent.

That is the way you should be for several reasons. First, it is your money. Why would you throw it away? What is more important-having a financially stable company or being broke yet having the respect of a teenage internet mark? If they were so smart, they wouldn't need to feel important by being critical of you anyway. They are irrelevant. I think it will say a lot about you and your character if you delay shows based on monetary issues rather than screwing wrestlers so you can afford to operate your wrestling franchise.

Take your time. Wise companies in any field only do business when profit seems to be in their favor.

I have found that every promoter and every owner has experienced several financial setbacks. Despite the threat of collapse, most are determined to succeed. Why ? Wrestling is fun. There is nothing like a group of rabid fans coming to see your work of art. Profit is icing on the cake. Whether it is you the promoter or you the owner, you the human being will enjoy the action.

Unless there is an owner in your area who has well documented integrity, personal ownership is probably the most viable approach. This is why the majority of the book is written in the context that both duties are resting squarely on your shoulders.

You can do well in wrestling if you have the same attitude as you would with any business. Pick up as much knowledge as you can, don't risk everything on one deal, and take your time to make the important decisions.

Promoters and owners are becoming scarce in the business. Large amounts of money are being lost during these economic times. Let's take a look at the fate of pro wrestling and why you might not want to worry about trends on a national scale.

Pro wrestling's popularity is bound to flow like a faucet. Sometimes revenue and fan interest explodes like a geyser while at other times, you can only hear the faint tap of a trickle of cash. Then, there are times you are in debt to the plumber.

Don't look at this as a crap shoot in Vegas, you are in this for the long haul. Don't panic but go slow. Take your time to develop your business.

Wrestling on a national scale runs hot and cold. In my opinion, that shouldn't affect local promotions. Even if the dominant wrestling powerhouse were to close their brass doors, wrestling is such an important piece of American culture that I do not think it will ever gasp its' last breath. There will always be fans with nostalgia in their hearts even if those numbers dwindle.

Five years ago, wrestling was in a huge upswing that I like to call the ECW factor. Competition between three companies caused wrestling to become interesting again. Competition is good and the more wrestling companies that develop their own stars helps ratings and interest for everyone. Many wrestling fans wanted to see Hulk Hogan in the WWF and Ric Flair in WCW so they watched both promotions.

This is true with indy wrestling. Don't let your competition discourage you. It could help you. Just develop what you have. You may be using some of their wrestlers so you will need some other edge to win. Be creative with how you use them in your show.

Can the WWE keep recycling ideas and stay atop as ratings king? Already, we are seeing a slide in their popularity and since the collapse of WCW and ECW, there has never been the kind of ratings or ticket and merchandise sales since then. The WWE's 'win' could be their ultimate downfall.

From the viewpoint of an indy promoter, that might not be a bad thing. Many indy promotions are passed over by the average fan because they can't identify with the wrestlers—they are not on tv therefore, they haven't heard of them. You can't sell a wrestler or his gimmick if the fans do not know them. Television seems to validate a wrestler in the mind of many fans and they make a connection with him or her. So, right now, you are a shadow to the WWE but if the WWE slides, the fans will look elsewhere.

Either way, you can make it.

Herein lies a truth, there are no guarantees in wrestling. Nobody has a 'get rich quick' answer (run from a promoter who says he does). However, there are certain tools and concepts in any industry which will help your chances of success. Learn the tools of marketing and small business administration and you will reap benefits accordingly.

Business laws are different in every state and tend to change rapidly. Use advice here as a template and not as an absolute. Your research is essential.

Chapter 4

Opening Bell: The first things you should do

Now, you are ready to live your dream. You've weighed your decision and have decided to step between the ropes and face the challenge. It may seem overwhelming when considering where to start.

The first step is to develop a plan that will work for you. Assuming that you are the owner of the next great wrestling promotion and not just the promoter, you need to pay a visit to City Hall. There, you need to fill out the necessary paperwork and pay the necessary fees for the processing of your business license.

This is the first thing you need to do and it must be done at least two months before your first event. Most cities have to publish the name of your company in a publication and for at least 30 days the license is on hold. California requires you to get a business license in each city that you perform in so make sure you ask how far your license extends when doing business as a wrestling company in your area.

Despite the fact that I've seen shows that were promoted without the proper licensing, it eventually caught up with them and they were shut down (sometimes on the night of the event). Fines are received by violators and a stern warning not to attempt another show without a license.

You also need to look into the Athletic Commission in your state. As of this writing, the only two states where the Athletic Commission charges a fee is Nevada and New York.

That doesn't mean that they won't still show up to try to collect some money. To describe the situation more fully, here's something Ric Drasin once wrote in an article which appeared on his webpage:

> Later in the 80's after Vince McMahan declared wrestling as entertainment and got rid of the Athletic commission in California, I started running more shows under the name American Wrestling Federation at Strongbow Stadium in Bakersfield. I picked Bakersfield because it has the oldest standing arena in the round. It's a masterpiece of nostalgia and should be picked up by movie studios as it's got a lot of history and great atmosphere to run shows. I really had no problem at this point with shows as the Olympic Auditorium was out of business, there was no NWA out here and basically no competition. But the commission did show up and asked for tax on the show, or they'd close me down. I told them to take a hike...and leave. They had no jurisdiction. They said that now they wanted Entertainment tax. What ? Leave or I'll throw you out. They left, sent me a bill about 2 weeks later. I sent it back and said 'stick it' and never heard from them again. I knew my rights !

Drasin was inspired to write this article from an experience that I had at my wrestling event. A man named Bobby Ponce showed up from the California Athletic Commission and tried to collect money but got lost in the shuffle. I never saw him after the show. I was 'warned' by Kirk White that "Bobby" might be at the show. It's strange how Kirk would know that. It was really interesting because Kirk White who had rented the ring to me claimed that he had never met Bobby Ponce. Yet, my brother had remembered seeing Mr. Ponce at a Big Time Wrestling show (of which, Mr. White is the promoter). So, I always wondered what Mr. White and Mr. Ponce's relationship was.

Mike Modest, who owns and wrestles for Pro Wrestling Iron as well as wrestling in Japan for Pro Wrestling NOAH, sent me the following information about the Athletic Commission:

> They no longer regulate professional wrestling here in California. They still regulate it in many states but not here. However occasionally they will show up and try to collect. What we have done in the past to get them off our backs is write them a check and then stop payment or tell them they will have to wait until the end of the show in which case they usually leave and then we never send the check. One time we just told them to wait and they did then we told them very politely that we know they no longer regulate pro wrestling. It is not a sport. Sports entertainment.

Another thing you'll need to look into is liability insurance. You can buy liability insurance for the year or per event. Of course, which you choose should be dependent on how many shows you intend to run in a year. The more you run, the more it would make sense to get the insurance for the year. Most buildings will tell you how much insurance they require and some can even point out local insurers who they are comfortable recommending. Smaller buildings and venues will ask for a million dollars in liability insurance while a larger auditorium may ask two million dollars. These 'policies' will run you a couple hundred dollars (I saw you checking your wallet for that elusive million dollar bill).

Business licenses, athletic commissions, and liability insurance. You can begin to see that it's not as easy as just setting up a ring in an auditorium and opening the doors. It may also be a good stroke of common sense to touch base with an attorney. He can tell you how to set up your business and how to avoid legal woes. I never had an attorney for advice and I did fine but it's better to make the proper connections before help is needed.

Something else to consider in this process is the use of a

good ticket agency. Ticketmaster, www.ticketmaster.com , is the biggest. Most of the ticket agencies will offer the ease of ordering tickets from their webpage, advertising your show on their hotline, monthly advertisement fliers which filter through typical teenage haunts (music stores, coffee shops, bookstores and college campuses). Usually these ticket 'sales pitches' are included in the cost and will draw a few to your show.

A similar ticket service to Ticketmaster is www.tickets.com (usually called Tickets.com in the media). You won't have to worry about this at this point since you probably will not be renting a 'stadium' sized venue but many arenas already have agreements with one service or the other. In other words, a band touring in one city has to use Ticketmaster and in another city they use Tickets.com based upon the arena's agreement (sort of like not being able to order Coke OR Pepsi at a fast food establishment due to the fact that they have made a deal with one or the other). Again, this shouldn't be a problem for a smaller show. You can use either.

Just like the aforementioned items were extremely positive reasons for using professional ticketing services, there is a downside to using them also. For one thing, many of the agencies charge your customers an additional handling fee beyond the cost of the ticket. So, usually fans of your show will purchase the tickets at the event to avoid the extra cost. This provides a lot of anxiety to a promoter who cannot anticipate the evening's turnout. This has always been a problem with using these companies. Also, these companies require you to pay an initial 'membership' type of fee. It may not be an obscene amount of money but hey, you're probably trying to pinch pennies as it is to present the best show possible.

Pro Wrestling Iron uses a 'credit card charging' website like the ones used by the internet auction sites. In fact, they use the one that Ebay uses (and now owns), PayPal (www.paypal.com). They are the biggest and they are very user friendly. Your fans would have no problem accessing and completing the transaction providing they know the basics of web surfing. The downside of this type of ticket distribution is that unlike the ticket agencies, the baton of responsibility is yours as you track ticket requests and mail them to your customers. You lose a little bit of advertising that the agencies provide but you can use the money you save to spread the word yourself.

Many wrestling promotions make connections with music stores, comic book shops, sporting goods stores, etc., and all their tickets are sold through them. Usually there is some type of percentage that the establishment receives for every ticket sold. The handling fees that are collected by the ticket agencies are eliminated using this method but it also removes the ease with which your fans can order. They now have to drive, walk or bike to a destination to purchase their event pass. If your audience is primarily young and lacks an engine which propels them down the street, this could be an obstacle.

Again, this may be another opportunity for observance. Look around your area and see how other wrestling companies are selling their tickets. What is working for their promotions? This will give you a good idea of what your fans expect and will maximize ticket sales as you alter your services accordingly.

Following these Chicken Gutless steps (I wondered how I'd sneak the title into this chapter), you now have a business license, liability insurance, ticket services, etc. Your next step should be to view the competition.

Promoters from other states may be more willing to share ideas but you don't want to waste your money 'frequent flying' to see how other regional companies are doing it. In addition, companies outside of your sphere of influence won't give you a clear picture of fans in your area. So, most of your local observations will be done incognito as a paying customer. Pay attention to how the crowd reacts to matches, show ambiance, etc. What did they like? What did you like? What could you improve upon? Better yet, what could you offer that would be unique and appealing?

Advertising is a very important part of event promotions. While you are working on all of the groundwork, begin to collect information on ways to publicize your matches. The best and most creative ways to market your product are cheap or sometimes free. Everything else will eat into your budget. We will discuss that in greater detail in the next chapter.

An excellent way to increase your spending money or budget is to seek out sponsorship. Sponsorship can be manifest through many arrangements based on your ingenuity and sales ability. Usually, you will be giving something in return such as advertising at the event. For example, a local restaurant may give you money in return for a page in your wrestling program and/or an announcement during the event over the public address system. Obviously, the more they contribute, the more publicity they'll be receiving from you during the show. Several companies have gone with a system that rewards graduated sponsor amounts of monetary compensation in exchange for graduated event advertising, i.e. $500 for a page in your wrestling program and $1,000 for a poster size ad hanging up in the lobby and free tickets for their employees. Other forms of recognition are advertisements around the ring apron, freebie gifts with their company logo on them, etc. The ideas are only limited to what you can brainstorm and achieve.

Sometimes local bottling companies will sponsor your event for the opportunity to sell their tasty beverage at your event. You get revenue. They get revenue and promotion. Coke, Pepsi and Budweiser are among the big bottling plants. However, if you are doing a fundraiser at a school, they might want you to seek sponsorship from Coke or Pepsi as opposed to Budweiser. Always be aware of your target audience as well as the tastes of the folks who are renting you the building or auditorium.

Another idea is to set up an autograph session at a comic book shop, sports memorabilia store, shopping mall, or car lot for an agreed upon sponsorship amount. To give you an example, Mark in Canada would collect $500 from his local shopping mall for a Honky Tonk Man and Iron Sheik autograph session. The two wrestlers charged $5 per autograph (on an 8 x 10 photo- which the wrestlers supplied). The wrestlers kept the fan's money, Mark kept the mall's capital contribution, and the mall had several hundred wrestling fans under their roof for an hour. This is also built in publicity for the wrestling company because the autograph session took place the day of the event which meant that Mark was able to pass out fliers alluding to the event and both wrestlers were not flown in only for the mall appearance thereby eliminating extra costs.

I had heard that one promoter in the Bay Area who negotiates many autograph sessions in Northern California has actually conned companies out of even more money. How does he do this? He has charged the sponsoring company for airfare to bring the wrestler to town. Unbeknownst to the owner or management of the establishment (who may not really be wrestling fans), the wrestler was brought to town on the WWF's dollar as part of a national tour. This is unacceptable fraud and definitely not recommended by me. The past will always catch up to you eventually.

I might also be digressing a bit but this same promoter asks the wrestlers to get him free t shirts from the WWF (now known as WWE) so that he can sell them to his customers. This was told to me by the Honky Tonk Man. I'm telling you that when your fans know you are ripping them off, you will pay dearly. Walk away from temptations to earn money the "easy way". The consequences outweigh the benefits.

When contacting sponsors, it is best to remember that they are professionals. Therefore, speak their language and behave as they behave. Buy business cards and letterhead, dress suitably for appointments and speak eloquently and appropriately. Also, these people have never seen you before, act confidently. If they turn you down, be polite and approach the next potential sponsor. You never know when you will meet again so don't burn your bridges.

It is about this time that you need to set up a webpage for your company. Fans need to be able to access your site for news. There are many ways to set up a domain name and to find internet pages offering web hosting. Even popular websites like Yahoo offer different pricing plans through their web hosting services at www.geocities.com. You can also set up a website reasonably at www.tripod.com. All you really need to do is put the words "domain name" and "web hosting" into your favorite search engine and you will find a large array of services. One way to register a domain name is at www.domain.com.

Every credible wrestling company is on the internet. You should consider it, also. If nothing else, the website should list upcoming shows (where they will be held, the time of the event, how to get to the building, the cost of tickets, who will be on the show, etc.). Extra features could be roster profiles (get the fans connected to your wrestlers), recap of previous shows, message board, etc.

Good examples of wrestling company websites include www.americanwrestlingfederation.com, www.prowrestlingiron .com, www.mlw.com. No one expects a brand new company to 'wow' them with a stand out website but as long as you get some information to your fans, you will be doing some critical work. However, an impressive webpage will get more attention.

Another smart move on the web is to make contact with the webmasters at the wrestling news sites. Submit news and 'press releases' to these webpages. A great wrestling website with lots of hits (unique visitor visits) is www.theturnbuckle.com. The webmaster is Ryan Timm.

Other wrestling websites that should be able to accommodate your news briefs and press releases are www.wrestlingunlimited.com, www.ewrestling.com, www.prowrestling.com, and www.wrestlingdotcom.com. Remember, if anyone should ever give you negative press, react in a controlled fashion. Take criticism constructively because you need to keep these channels open. If nothing else, try to work with each 'critic' on the internet. They may become your friends. It is a weird business, after all.

You can also release news about upcoming events to the sparse collection of wrestling newspaper columnists that exist. Two of the big ones are Blackjack Brown of the Chicago Sun-Times and the Slammer at the New York Daily News. The Slammer wears a mask (only in wrestling would a newspaper columnist take a publicity photo with a mask on). He has no email but you can send your news to: The Slammer, Daily News,

Sports Dept., 450 West 33 Street, New York, NY 10001. Cody Monk writes a column for the Dallas Morning News and can be reached at cmonk@dallasnews.com

Here comes the fun part which is the use of the 'Vulcan mind meld' to communicate with the Neanderthal brutes that are known as WRESTLERS. I'm kidding, of course. Wrestlers today do not always fit the stereotype of the past. Many of them are college graduates and have previously been employed in all walks of life. Most indy wrestlers that you meet on the circuit have a primary job outside of the pros.

This is the time to pull out that budget and do some heavy consultation with your faux leather checkbook! After this convergence of logical thought and financial number crunching, you should have a price range that you are able to live with without shedding small waterfalls of pained perspiration. Words of advice: you can overpay wrestlers, you can also spend too much in general. At this phase, your preparation might simply be to create a notebook with each wrestler's price range and ability. You can get some "good deals" out there so do your homework!

Also, do not commit to anyone at this point. Give yourself a good 3 to 4 months before your first show to lay the groundwork. Patiently deciding who will fit into your show will take some time and a little observation.

It is good advice to view every wrestler in action so that you know what their skill level is. Don't just ask a wrestler about his abilities because he is selling himself to your company. He's not going to tell you he is under trained. What man or woman on a blind date describes themselves in less than flattering terms? If this person is local, view them in action. If they are inquiring about work and they live outside your area, most of them will be happy to send a video of their previous matches.

You will be surprised at how fast word will spread in the wrestling community that you are looking for workers. Even before you began, they were looking for you.

Some of the best indy wrestlers can be found on the internet. Among them are: Mike Modest and Donovan

Morgan at www.prowrestlingiron.com, Christopher Daniels at www.christopherdaniels.com, and the Ballard Brothers at www.ballardbrothers.net. Also, many older superstars have set up webpages including: www.thehonkytonkman.com, www.ultimatewarrior.com, www.machoman.com, and www.nativetatanka.com. It is getting easier to make contact with professional wrestlers.

A word of caution on the employment of wrestlers, if you do not contact each individual you will be hiring directly and have to go through another promoter, that promoter will probably charge you enough to make a sizable profit themselves. This may not happen if they forward your requests to the wrestler but there is a good chance that you are being taken if they act as the intermediary.

Here are two examples from my experience working with promoters on contacting talent. Keep in mind that these business dealings are with two separate people from two different regions of the country.

I had contacted the Suicide Kid in Southern California through an unscrupulous owner. This business man, who was once a longtime WWF referee, charged me $150 for Suicide to do my show. The show ended up being cancelled but I was committed to compensating the wrestlers since they had set that date aside. I sent the $150 to the owner, care of "Suicide Kid" Mikey Henderson. Later, when I needed to use the Suicide Kid again, I spoke to him directly. I asked him if the promoter had paid him $150 and he informed me that he was only given $50. I immediately sent him the difference. Two weeks later, I received $100 from the promoter with an apology. Apparently, the two of them had had a discussion in lieu of the development.

I once tried to track down an elusive yet famous wrestler. He was elusive because his family was trying to find him due to missed child support payments. So, I finally found a company in Texas who was using this man on a regular basis. I made a connection with the 'top dog' in their talent relations and he confirmed that he knew the whereabouts of Jake "The Snake"

Roberts. Sensing that I was a new promoter (and apparently very naïve), he used the ever popular bait and switch tactic. He offered me another former WWF mainstay Doink the Clown for $500 plus airfare and hotel.

Doink the Clown was a superstar in the WWF. That much was a fact. However, the inside joke in indy wrestling was that there were now "Doinks" in every state. Despite the WWF's attempts to shut down the imposters, the impersonations thrived due to the fact that each wrestler was covered up in a clown costume and no identification of authenticity on the part of the fans was possible. None of these bozos (or Doinks) were an original Doink, just a little known jobber in a clown suit. The price of $500 would have been an incredible and shameless scam.

If you have a unique idea in wrestling, don't give it away so easily. I've made that mistake, too. I once contacted Ted DiBiase with the idea of starting a 'family oriented' wrestling program. Don't get me wrong, the wrestling would be treated seriously. All of the soap opera aspects of the WWE would be eliminated. DiBiase must have loved it because he forwarded my email to his agent, Joe Alessi. I called Mr. Alessi at his request and we talked about shopping the idea around to some family friendly cable networks that might be interesting in supporting the idea.

The reason why I thought of Ted DiBiase was due to the fact that I knew that he was of the same religious faith as I am. So, I felt that he would have the same desire to be responsible to content, his name recognition would add some credence to the company, and that he would be trustworthy.

As I was doing this, the WXO was formed. Imagine my shock as I watched Ted DiBiase as commissioner of "wrestling your whole family can watch". The WXO didn't last because they didn't really treat it seriously. Their idea of a promo was a fat guy trying to get out of a little car. Now, I may be dumb but even I know that doesn't sell. I am not saying that my idea was stolen because I do not know that. I'm saying that I would have made a wiser decision by keeping the idea to myself.

I've also heard of indy wrestlers who sent videos to the WWE with new holds and gimmicks. They were never hired but their idea was used and of course, they were never compensated. Again, I do not know but that the WWE was already aware or had that gimmick in mind. Still, it's safer to keep your ideas to yourself if they can benefit you.

Further proof that the business is littered with trash or as one indy wrestler once put it," Everybody in wrestling calls each other brother and then stabs them in the back."

Amen, brother.

Chapter 5

Preliminary Bouts- Getting Organized, Getting Ready

The easiest mistake you can make when promoting your first match is either spending too much or too little money. Usually the blunder most often made is the former and it almost always depletes the company bankroll in devastating fashion.

Smart promoting means longevity in the wrestling universe. This takes a great amount of planning and a generous measure of common sense, too. You need to spend time figuring out a budget that guarantees survival and the ability to organize another event. Use a percentage breakdown that works for you but here's the one I use:

Wrestlers	33%
Venue	33%
Advertising	8-10%
Other Expenses	25%

Let's see how to factor this with real numbers. Let's say you have $2,400 to spend on the show. If you have 161 fans paying $15 each, you have a miniscule profit of $15. Your totals would be the following:

Wrestlers	$800
Venue	$800

| Advertising | $200 |
| Other Expenses | $600 |

How many wrestlers do you need for a show? You can probably get by with ten wrestlers at a minimum. This will give you five matches plus a battle royal with all ten. Add a twenty minute intermission to sell sodas, snacks and merchandise and you have a suitable two hour (or more) extravaganza.

A very important subject to be brought up before the event takes place is liability. I'm not referring to liability insurance in this case but something that walks hand in hand with your policy. By now, you should already have the insurance. However, it is also important to have each wrestler sign a waiver of liability. It might be important to have this added protection. After all, how difficult is it to fake an injury and sue in today's society? Besides, any experienced wrestler who has performed for established indy promotions has seen his or her share of waivers. I wholeheartedly believe in fair compensation for wrestlers but I also keep in mind that all risks are taken by voluntary decisions of the ring warriors. A waiver can be a sheet of paper like this:

> I, (put wrestler's name here), sign this waiver that I will not hold (name of your wrestling company) responsible for any injuries as a result of my actions during the wrestling event on (date of event). By signing this, I am acknowledging that I take full responsibility for any monetary loss I experience due to medical care as a result of injury. I am also stating that I will not seek legal action against (name of your wrestling company) if such injuries occur.

> _____   _____
> (Date)   (signature of wrestler)

You are now officially a business, you are able to offer tickets, you have a budget, and you are ready to book your first show. Where will you hold your first event?

There are many venues to consider. The most expensive are the auditoriums and civic centers. They usually will seat the most people, also.

In the beginning, this type of building is probably not a good idea. You have to build a loyal fanbase and develop some contacts before taking on this kind of responsibility. Even longstanding, well respected indy promotions avoid the financial commitment of a large auditorium. On the rare occasion that they do book a sizable event, they usually feel compelled to book a minimum of two nationally recognized wrestlers (usually former WWE and WCW superstars) which creates an enormous show budget and an incredible gamble. In short, a new promoter or, more specifically, company with no long term positive publicity is taking too big of a risk. I do not recommend it. There are a lot of hidden costs in these type of buildings such as security, lighting operators, sound system operators, etc.

There are other venues which would be more prudent to rent. Most counties have a fairground and many of them have different size facilities with various price ranges. I have not found the county fair location in my area to be very reasonable in price. Also, you have to march past the front gate, past several exhibit halls, over a long lawn area to arrive at the show. It is quite a distance to get to the venue. These are things to consider and not every fairground is the same.

The city parks usually have recreation centers to rent. They are usually pretty reasonable in price. I also know a few promoters who have events at American Legion Halls, Veterans of Foreign Wars centers, and Masonic Temples. One promoter was doing a lot of crazy hardcore matches like exploding barbed wire and flaming tables. They kicked him to the curb. What's the lesson to be learned? Don't lose a venue by burning your tables. Don't upset those who are allowing you to rent the building.

Despite the fact that there was a history of territories in pro wrestling, there are no territorial borders today. Promoters will sometimes tell you that there are (at least they tried that with me). Don't believe it. Gas stations compete across the street with each other. You have every right to promote wherever you would like to promote. You even have a right to underbid them when attempting to do fundraisers that they already have agreements with. As long as you are not operating dishonestly, these are business practices used everywhere in every type of business. In other words, don't lie to the charity to get their work, just offer something better.

If they can't roll with the pack, they'll just fall behind. Think of it this way, if they are dishonest, you may be offering that charity a better solution.

Any place that you book on your own and promote on your own, the profits are yours. However, as mentioned earlier, you also have the option of offering and organizing fundraiser wrestling events.

The disadvantage of a fundraiser is that the profits are not all yours. However, the advantages are many. First, you are giving some of the money collected to a good cause. Second, most organizations you will be working with will have some type of hall or gym. This eliminates the cost of renting a building. Third, you will probably have several extra helpers selling tickets. For example, if you were doing a show for a youth group, the young people could be enlisted to sell tickets to their friends and family. This creates great publicity for your company. Everyone benefits by the arrangement. Once you've established a good reputation and a pattern of trustworthiness, other fundraising opportunities are sure to follow.

I know one promoter who sells fundraiser event tickets for high schools at $12. Of that price, $2 goes to the school per ticket. So, if your promotion and their promotion can sell 500 tickets, they've made $1,000 on their efforts. That's not too bad for one fundraising event. I've noticed recently in this area that fundraising wrestling events are starting to be priced at $20 since the WWE's prices have skyrocketed. If the fans are accepting those prices in your area, there will be greater profit for your event for both parties.

Fundraising possibilities are endless. Look around your

community. You should have the typical YMCA locations, Boys and Girls Clubs, and schools.

There is another option when creating a wrestling spectacular. This would be to sell a show outright. County fairs look to dispense currency on entertainment as an extra draw for people to spend money on an admission ticket. Sports clubs such as minor league baseball sometimes try to attract more fans with special postgame entertainment. The same can be said for conventions, car lots and shopping malls. Be creative in your search for ways to get the exposure. Send out a professional brochure to as many organizations and companies who may be interested. Make sure that your price is competitive yet profitable. My cover letter went something like this (keep in mind, this was geared toward shopping malls but received a call from a car dealership based upon the mailing):

> We've got one of the best promotional events that you could dream of, a live pro wrestling show. Wrestling is being used across the country for fundraisers and promotional events with amazing results. Sellouts everywhere they appear. It's an excellent way to reach your customers.
>
> We supply the ring, wrestlers, timekeeper, referee, photos for publicity, announcer and the show consisting of 5 great matches. You supply the building or tent and security. Great for a parking lot or center court. You can sell tickets inside the mall shops and we will provide a program to each of the fans with coupons good for these shops. In addition, each of the stores and the information booth can sell the tickets for $10 and we will only take $8.

Next, contact your wrestlers. You should already have a notebook to reference salaries and wrestler ability. You want a good mixture of wrestlers. This would include heavyweights (large, muscular wrestlers), cruiserweights (smaller, high flying, technically sound athletes), and larger than life warriors (colorful, eye catching gimmick wrestlers).

If you feel that you need a well known wrestler to attract an audience, check out their rates. Also, most "big name" superstars require a 'deposit' which is usually 50% of their salary up front. They also typically require airfare and hotel. For instance, from my location in California, the Honky Tonk Man is a better buy than King Kong Bundy. Why? Assuming they would want the same price, Honky has a shorter distance to fly to California than King Kong Bundy who resides on the East Coast. Also, Bundy asked for two airline seats due to his size. So, there are a lot of expenses when dealing with the well known talent.

Bad for them but good for you, their prices seem to be on the decline since the ranks of unemployed wrestlers rose with the collapse of WCW and ECW. What about hiring a former ECW star vs. an older WWF star? Let's suppose that their salary requests are comparable. In this case, my opinion is to hire the older WWF wrestler. My feeling is that even if it is a former ECW performer from the late '90s, his exposure to fans will still be far less than someone who has been in the World Wrestling spotlight. This rule is not set in stone and will often be dependent on demographics, etc.

Most of your wrestlers of the indy variety will be unrecognizable to a majority of fans since a large percentage of them are exclusively wrestling on the circuit and are not getting any television time. So, from that pool of available talent, you want to make sure they are local. Regardless if a tag team is extremely skilled, if nobody has heard of them (which equals no drawing power) it makes no sense to eat away your budget on wasted airfares and hotel rooms which are added to their salary. Hire local grapplers as much as possible and your wallet will be much obliged.

Through phone calls and emails, you have a roster of bruisers and brawlers. A few babyfaces in there and you have the makings of great drama and high adventure. You must now purchase the necessary equipment that is standard to wrestling shows in order to make their adventures attainable.

Here's an idea, let's start first with their domain, which is also known as the ring. If you or someone you know is mechanically inclined far beyond Barney Fife or even yours truly, you can consider purchasing ring plans. Ring plans are sold everywhere on the internet, particularly on auction sites. Although most of the prices are cheap, you usually receive a third or fourth generation copy from the 'quick buck' seller. It is my opinion that many of these plans are ambiguous but might be useful in formulating an idea of what you need to build your championship ring.

Rings come in sizes of 16' x 16', 18' x 18' and 20' x 20'. The smallest size is suitable for indy wrestling. Plans require welding so keep in mind that you will need a professional. When purchasing the necessary pieces to build the ring (i.e. cables, bolts, wood), make sure that they are strong enough to maintain the weight that will be placed upon them. Most hardware stores would have the capacity limits listed of these items.

The ropes on a wrestling ring are internally comprised of steel cable. The most common way to make the ropes is to thread the cable through a garden hose, then cover the hose with tape. It is important to make sure that you are doing this properly as a rope break can cause serious injuries.

When attaching the ropes to the ring, you can either buy twelve turnbuckles (the hook and eye variety) for each rope and each corner or buy six turnbuckles for two of the ringposts and use chains on the other two. It's cheaper and it will not be noticeable if you have covers.

If your fear is that your hand/eye coordination impairs you from creating anything but a metal heap resembling a pile up on the Jersey turnpike, then buying an existing wrestling ring is your option. There are different ways to go depending on what websites you explore. Sometimes you can buy just the frame or some webpages sell used rings. A word on used rings: there is a long line of unsatisfied customers who have bought used ring equipment without seeing it firsthand. I once bought a title belt on EBay. The belt looked brand new in the picture but when I received it, it was well worn with missing snaps and torn leather. A huge purchase such as a wrestling ring which will probably cost you a few thousand dollars should be seen in person. However, the majority of squared circles for sale are new. Therefore, it will take a measure of shrewdness to discover the best deal.

There are many rings for sale over the internet. Here are three sites that sell rings: www.masterbuiltboxingrings.com , www.1wrestlinglegends.com/mypicks/mpring.htm, and www.p rowrestlingrings.com . Be patient, compare prices and ask for references if you still aren't satisfied.

There is also the option of renting the ring of a neighboring promotion. If you can find a competing company that will be fair with you, then this may be a temporary solution for your lack. Make sure you get the rental cost in writing because many owners have been known to 'up' the price minutes before setting up the ring. As you can see, this is not necessarily the best option but it is an option.

If you are renting the ring from a training school, sometimes they will give you a deal for using their students. Training schools are dying to give their "boys" exposure in the ring.

Just like with wrestling rings, plans and portions (i.e. leather belts, metal plates) of ring belts are sold on auction sites and all over the net. You can also get a pretty good deal on used title belts on the web. I suppose used title belts for sale on the internet is a bit like dating through the internet. There is a great temptation to show the belt during better years, with less wear and tear than the present wounds that scar it. However, if you want a professional championship belt, you may want to contact a legendary belt maker, Reggie Parks. Mr. Parks has made belts for all the major companies including the NWA. Reggie's website is located at http://www.midwestwrestling.com/ Beltentrance.htm. J Mar belts, who have made belts for the WWF, are located at www.beltster.com. Check out www.cham pionshipleather.com, too.

There are other items that may not necessarily be deemed essential such as ring bell, event programs, merchandise (i.e.

t-shirts, posters) can be purchased with any funds that are amazingly still existent after your large expenditures. Nobody knows how you did it and you might entertain writing your own book!

If you've already lined up some sponsors, then you are probably compelled to print a wrestling event program which features the bouts, insider information, small articles on wrestlers and your sponsor's advertisement. Those sponsors have paid the printing or copying costs. The beauty of it is that you can turn around and sell each program, resulting in a profit. If you are unsure about t-shirt sales initially (and that's a legitimate concern since this will be your first try) and cannot afford the risk of printing up a reasonable quantity, your next best option is to advertise t-shirts in the event program. Explain that they can be ordered on the website. In this regard, you can gauge how many you need to make as the orders arrive.

Event programs can be made in small quantities without a printing press these days. Most programs are simply black and white documents. Many corner copy centers such as Kinko's have Xerox Docutechs and Digipaths which are large copiers that can actually manipulate the originals, create halftones, and layout the artwork on 11 x 17 inch paper. 11x 17 makes a good size for a program. They can be folded down to a standard sheet of paper and stapled in the middle. By coincidence, I know a wrestling student in Southern California by the name of Clayton Taylor who works for Kinko's. I mention this because he was one of the first to buy the original No Chicken Guts for the Wrestling Soul. I figured he deserved the mention.

If you noticed, I mention a lot of people in this book. Please do this as a promoter. Give credit where credit is due. Do not make yourself the center of attention. Ronald Reagan once said," You can do anything you want to do as long as you don't mind who gets the credit." The Bible (specifically Paul) says it like this, "Though I am free from all men, I make myself a servant and gain the more." You will thrive and build lasting friendships if you allow your ego to take a backseat. Make your business their business. If you do this, they will be loyal. Give praise and give it sincerely.

Now, there needs to be some type of trumpet call or writing in the sky to alert the legion of wrestling fanatics of your arrival. That trumpeting can be accomplished through a medley of various forms of media. Which ones work in your area may take another look at your competition and some sound thinking on your part.

In other words, if television advertising is an option for you, you wouldn't want to place a commercial for the upcoming 'BrutalFest' during a woman's 'grab your kleenex' talk show. Yet, you might want to have a commercial at halftime of the local college football game. Most of the sales reps who represent the television stations and cable tv will be trying to accommodate you but you will be the one who is most aware of how your commercial can be best utilized. For instance, my local cable representative was not aware of the wrestling time slots and I had to point them out. So, targeting your audience will be of extreme importance when not wanting to waste dollars in your budget.

Forms of media that you can employ may be different from community to community. Let's take a look at television advertising first.

Television is probably the most expensive way to advertise. You can advertise on free tv or cable. I use cable to air my commercials. With cable, I was able to advertise in certain areas of the Bay Area during the Monday night wrestling shows. So, the costs were a fraction of the price tag for advertising with a local spot on network television, in particular UPN's Smackdown. In fact, one commercial on Smackdown was ten times the cost of one Monday night Raw advertisement. It would have been my entire budget for one thirty second spot. One thing I've learned, repetition is an invaluable tool. There will be a certain number of people who will not make the decision to go to your event until they've seen your commercial multiple times.

Radio is another good medium to present your product.

Just like television, you usually buy these commercials in bulk. Think about your audience. Are they listening to the local sports radio station? rock station? Hip hop? Give yourself time to identify your crowd. Think about young people and sports fans, and you will have a good idea where you need to advertise. Many of these stations will work with you on creative ideas. I've seen morning show disc jockeys and sports talk commentators participate as a guest ring announcer for the event. This is great publicity for your promotion and their radio station.

Interested in a creative way to have someone else pay for your advertising? Autograph sessions might be your answer (at least a part of it). As mentioned earlier, you can solicit sponsorship in return for an autograph session. Again, creativity in promoting is really a talent worth developing. The bonus to your creativity will be the reward you create for thinking outside of the box. Sponsorship doesn't have to be a cash exchange. In fact, it can be anything that you find to be mutually beneficial to both parties. I had a long conversation with the program manager of a local alternative rock music station. Our plan was to set up outside a nearby music store where they sold tickets on the day my show's tickets went on sale. I would bring a couple of wrestlers to greet the crowd while the radio station would bring attention to the gathering and would publicize the ticket information over their airwaves, in addition to passing out their bumper stickers. No money was exchanged between us but we both reaped the benefits.

The least expensive way to advertise your event is the use of posters and fliers. Don't sell this aspect of your marketing plan short (unless it's a midget wrestling event). Some footwork will be required on your part or the part of those who may be enlisted for help. Where are effective locations to disperse your leaflets? If there is a nearby university or college, there ought to be a few bulletin boards and wrestling fans congregated there. They also usually have a college radio station, too. You might want to offer discounts to groups of 20 or more and target the fraternity houses.

Many music stores have areas within their enterprise that

have piles of fliers featuring information on local bands and other entertainment. If possible, pass out your ads outside sports events and concerts. Also, it might be a good idea to target telephone poles and cars in parking lots. In short, the more who see your descriptive handout, the higher percentage of opportunities for tickets to be sold.

Be creative and be tireless in your efforts to find your audience. You will not get another chance once the event is over. You will never feel the pangs of regret for working 'too hard' in promoting your show.

Chapter 6

Pinfalls and Submissions- Strength in Numbers

Vital to your success, other promoters and volunteers must be sought out. Their help will be indispensable. Make sure that they share your vision and enthusiasm. Also, it is important to solicit the help of trustworthy helpers.

Requests for help can be posted on internet wrestling boards and webpages. Also, college campuses might be a good place to post fliers for volunteers and employees. If you must pay, you will definitely need to pay entry level wages in order to make a profit.

A volunteer photographer and/ or videographer will be your first line of media offense. Pictures are needed for press releases, internet news and event programs. Videographers are essential to begin videotape sales or to submit footage via television programs. I know of one promoter in Southern California who made a deal with a national music chain to stock his videos in their stores. He sold 1,800 tapes in a short period of time.

Many indy promotions enlist the help of volunteers to form "street teams". Street teams pass out advertising fliers and contribute them to billboards, telephone poles, and anywhere that fans may be found. Street teams are usually composed of young, enthusiastic fans who want to be part of the fun. You might want to reward them by giving them backstage event passes.

The event will probably need more volunteers for jobs such as ticket takers, ring crew, ushers, and security. Filling this necessity with volunteers will help keep costs low. The most crucial of these titles is security and it must be stressed to each person that the safety of the audience is of the utmost importance. An untrained security staff is to your detriment and if you feel unsure of your volunteers, you might want to spend the extra money on a professional security company.

Also, money is a huge temptation for many young people. So, when you have volunteers handling the ticket sales, make sure they are trustworthy.

If you find yourself strapped for time or are grammatically challenged, find a student with good English skills to write and submit press releases for you. This is critical. You must get the word out to the fans. If you do designate someone for this task, make sure they email those wrestling news websites and submit the release to the local newspaper. Answer all the typical journalistic questions within the document (who, what, why, when where) when promoting the upcoming show.

The same can be said about your company webpage. If you can find a volunteer or volunteers, it will be a huge help. Also, if they can make the site interactive with a forum to engage wrestling fans, you will generate and sustain interest.

Volunteer yourself as a guest columnist for one of the wrestling websites. Better yet, if there is a local radio show that would let you do a five or ten minute segment on your promotion that would give you a great advantage.

Also, contribute event information to wrestling message boards. A very large wrestling message board is at www.topropetalk.com. Again, Ryan Timm was the one who showed me this page.

If you cannot financially compensate your volunteers, make sure that you reward them in some way so that they know their help is appreciated. It may be in giving them some sort of personal award or something that appears to be an exclusive and creative thank you.

The help of other promoters is also a very important

assistance you can acquire. Promoters will be equipped with the skills to double your sales power, your sponsorship levels and your bottom line (profits). Also, if you are able to attract a list of local sales talent, you can keep your company more active by splitting the shows amongst the individual promoters. Just make sure that any agreements are made before the day of the event.

The more, the merrier applies here.

Chapter 7

The Main Event-What will your audience experience?

A faint cry builds within the musty halls until there are intensely disturbing decibels of noise. The fans are getting restless, having endured work related stress, family squabbles, heavy traffic and finally, standing in the ticket line. They needed this carnival atmosphere to divert their mundane lives. Don't destroy the mood by making them wait too long. It's time to start the show as the house lights fade to black and the ring announcer stands at attention in the center of the ring.

The show is starting but what exactly the crowd will be a witness to is entirely in your hands. Again, this would assume that you have creative control over the evening's festivities and are more than just the promoter.

One way to spice up your event is in your presentation. Most wrestling companies have followed in the WWE's footsteps, albeit a downscaled, cheaper version, in the entrance music that blares during the wrestlers' grand entrances. On the indy level, most of the wrestlers will bring their own music on CD and it's mostly popular radio music that they feel identifies with their ring persona. It's not a bad idea to bring a few CD's of your own just in case someone has forgotten to bring their theme. Make sure that you have an adequate sound system to play the music. Don't be talked into going overboard on costly sound system rentals because usually the house system will be sufficient.

Also, additional lighting may be needed for your show. There should be a few sound and lighting companies in the area. You can look them up in the phone book or ask the venue if they have any recommendations. Many local businesses dealing in this area will have some experience with boxing/wrestling/kickboxing events. As with anything else, prices and services offered will vary. If the venue has lighting that will be ample for your show, then this is a wasted expenditure.

Different types of matches, also known as gimmick matches, will spark interest in your fans. Let's take a look at some of my favorites.

LUMBERJACK MATCH

The lumberjack match is usually the culmination of a feud. It is a match designed to settle longstanding issues between two warring parties. Despite the name, it has nothing to do with lumber (unless Jim Duggan is involved). In theory, the lumberjack match is supposed to have a definite winner to determine the victor in the drawn out battle. In the world of wrestling, nothing is definite especially when a hot feud is a monetary influx. Essentially, lumberjacks usually operate with a number of faces (good guys) and heels (bad guys) patrolling around ringside. Typically, for the sake of fairness, there is an equal number of faces and heels to keep things balanced. Their task is to keep the action in the ring until there is a decisive winner but heels will be heels and sometimes fights happen outside the ring. Sometimes these fights unfairly decide the match. Hence, yet another rematch must be planned. Did someone say cage match? There are so many outcomes from a match like this and even another feud can be advanced by the actions between the faces and heels outside the ring.

TRIPLE THREAT MATCH

The triple threat match is exactly as it sounds. The addition of a third man is meant to add a more unpredictable conclusion. Three wrestlers go at it in the ring and sometimes out of the ring. I've seen this match have an extended time limit by letting one wrestler bail outside the ring and enter into the action moments after another wrestler 'takes a break'. The advertising of this type of match (sometimes with a title belt involved) can create a lot of interest in an event. Many great cruiserweight bouts have been triple threat matches.

TAG TEAM MATCH

I've seen six, eight and ten man tag team matches but mostly, these matches consist of teams of two. A rule of thumb for most promoters is to have a minimum of one tag team match. This breaks up the monotony of one on one match ups. In my opinion, this match should include some high fliers and should be fast paced unless it is the main event and features some of your popular heavyweights teaming up in a unique bout. Many promoters have tag team champions on the indy level. There are several noteworthy tag teams in the indy ranks now such as the Road Warriors and the Bushwhackers.

BATTLE ROYAL

You will see a lot of Battle Royals on the independent circuit. A Battle Royal is when a large number of competitors are in the ring at once. I've seen it as high as 30 men in the ring at the same time. The objective of such a match is to eliminate opponents by throwing them over the top rope and to be the last one standing in the ring. Pinfalls or submissions won't do it in this match. This is a very popular match in indy wrestling because most wrestlers will work a battle royal in addition to his or her regular match for the same price. So, the promoter gets an extra match without paying out additional funds. Also, most experts will tell you that this type of match is much better live than televised so it is perfect for the smaller shows. The Royal Rumble is really a variation of the Battle Royal where participants enter the match every few minutes (usually two or three minutes). The wrestlers have drawn their number before the match to see when they will enter the Rumble. Like the Battle Royal, the Royal Rumble is not won by pinfall or submission. You must throw the others over the top rope to be the final wrestler and thereby, the winner of the Rumble. The upside is that the fans have no idea when their favorites will enter the ring. The downside is that it is never truly a Battle Royal in the purest sense. The chances are great that all the 'Rumblers' will not be in the ring at the same time.

LOSER LEAVES TOWN MATCH

This type of bout was more popular in the past. The theory was that when a wrestler felt that he had over saturated the local scene, it was time to move on down the road to another territory. This still could be a high exposure match particularly if you have a wrestler who wants to take some time off or is moving to another area. It is even better (at least for the wrestler) if the wrestler is going to the 'big time'. This is similar to the retirement match which can be used when a local talent has decided to hang up the wrestling boots.

TITLE MATCH

The title match is probably the most effective and climactic portion of your event. There are many types of titles in professional wrestling. Heavyweight Championships and Tag Team Championships seem to be the most popular. There are too many to mention here but a few of them are: Cruiserweight, Hardcore, State and Regional Champions. They often help to highlight the added importance of the match. Usually the titles are decided in the main event. Titles can assist in hyping your event and also in advancing storylines. It's all dependent on how you develop your bouts. One thing about titles, do not treat them as a joke. Keep these matches as serious displays of athleticism and your fans will respect your company and the title that represents it. It is a bad idea for an angle to give your title to a non-wrestler (like WCW did with actor, David Arquette).

FALLS COUNT ANYWHERE MATCH

With a Falls Count Anywhere match, enthusiasm is high with the anticipation that the action will spill out into the audience. The premise is that a pinfall is counted in or out of the ring. Make sure that your combatants keep a fair distance from the crowd or else some unplanned calamity may occur.

BRASS KNUCKLES/STEEL GLOVE MATCH

The Brass knuckles or steel glove match was the old school precursor to the modern day weapons match. This forerunner is a perfect example of how the sport has changed. One weapon was only deemed to be necessary as opposed to its' present successor (which is usually a bloody display with barbed wire baseball bats and metal objects). The brass knuckles, steel glove, cow bell, or various other weapons was usually placed on a pole in one of the corners. The wrestler who was able to subdue his opponent long enough to climb up to the top turnbuckle and up the pole was given a huge advantage with the help of the weaponry. This was a fun match that would still work well today.

There are many other great matches that you can book on your show. If you find yourself with lots of extra time and only one or two matches left to go, you might want to make one of them a two out of three falls match. What that means is that the winner of two out of three pinfalls is the one who takes the match. This can be a very dramatic and engaging contest.

If you are promoting the event near Halloween or you have a couple of creepy grapplers, a coffin match might be just what the doctor ordered (especially if that doctor's last name is Frankenstein). You can pick up cheap caskets on the internet. I know one promotion that got a pet store to donate a snake when Jake the Snake was in town so maybe a funeral home has an extra casket dying to be used. The winner of the casket match is the one who closes the coffin on his opponent.

Many promotions make up their own matches. Mark Anderson's Hardcore Wrestling Federation promoted a 'Kill the Clown' match with the omnipresent Doink the Clown. There were no stipulations to 'Kill the Clown' because there was really no such thing as a 'Kill the Clown' match. Why promote it like that? It generated interest. Interest generated ticket sales. After all, who can miss a 'Kill the Clown' match?

Also, promoters believe that the first match of the night should be fast and short. You don't want to bore the audience with a long and slow moving bout. You want to give them a quick burst of action to draw them into this fantasy world early. Detached fans make for a long agonizing night for the promoter. You may even hear the dreaded chants of "boring!", So, if you want to subscribe to fast action early, two good cruiserweights would fit the bill.

To guarantee that fans will return to your next event, it is wise to develop storylines or angles. Feuds are a big part of wrestling's great storylines. Everybody wants to see a rematch if one is warranted. Knowing when to end a feud that is cooling down in intensity will take some practice.

If wrestling is an art form, William Goldbergspeare would say," To bleed or not to bleed, that is the razor !"

In the mid-eighties, Eddie Mansfield and a few other disgruntled wrestlers broke kayfabe and began to reveal the act of blading. Blading or juicing is the term used for a wrestler opening himself up by cutting himself with a small razor, which is usually hid in his trunks or taped to his wrist or hands. For several years after that, you rarely saw a wrestler juice.

As time passed, the promoters saw blading as something the fans wanted to see again. They didn't see red but green as in money. Blood seemed to go well with hardcore. The act of bleeding is at all levels including indy wrestling. I have seen workers blade and receive no pay.

As a promoter, you have to decide if you want blading in your show or not as you will be the one setting up the action in the ring. Due to the fact that everyone knows what the wrestlers are doing when they are busted open and with HIV being all too real, I can't see a logical reason why blading is necessary. That's my opinion.

Once a wrestler has finished his performance in the ring, you will be paying him. Wrestlers like to be paid in cash. For one thing, most are wrestling on the weekend and on the road. This makes it difficult to cash a check then. There is a lot of mistrust in pro wrestling and I doubt anyone would take a personal or company check anyway. So, I usually have each wrestler's pay in sealed envelopes. You don't want the wrestlers to know who is getting paid what, particularly if there is a pay scale you use. Then, upon receipt of payment, I have them sign a paper that they were paid.

I would like to recommend a book that will give you a good legal perspective on professional wrestling. I have not seen another one like it. It is called "The Essential Legal Guide for the Professional Wrestler" written by Eric C. Perkins, ESQ. The publisher is 1st Books (www.1stbooks.com).

You now have the tools to make good choices when organizing your first event. Based upon your own experiences, you will be able to make proper adjustments.

Let's take a look at your future. You are now running regular shows, how can you expand your business?

Chapter 8

Beyond Promoting- Expanding your Opportunities

Congratulations, you are living your dream. They said you couldn't do it but you proved them wrong. That is an accomplishment alone when you consider most people take their dreams to the cemetery. Most have not dared to walk the path you've chosen. I can not promise you a pot of gold at the end of the rainbow but I can promise the rainbow.

If you are satisfied with your company doing shows and growth is not a necessity, then you might not want to seriously consider the ideas in this chapter. There's no need to stretch yourself beyond your interests. On the other hand, if you would like to explore what's beyond your initial success, press on.

At the point that shows are taking place on a regular basis, you may want to explore your growth. Fans come and go but a wise promoter will seek out new fans. One of the ways to accomplish this is through television.

Many companies start small by exposing television viewers to their live shows on cable access channels. The shows are usually filmed on cheap digital cameras, converted to eight millimeter and half hour segments are aired on the television station with free airtime. Eventually, the goal will be to sign up sponsors and televise your show on local television. This will also help to promote your live events and create recognition for your wrestlers.

As you become deeper entrenched in your community,

you will have greater opportunities for profit. Merchandise will be key to your financial success. A new webpage that seems to be working for fan clubs, music performers and indy wrestling organizations is www.cafepress.com. On this CafePress, you are able to upload your artwork or picture to display for selling t shirts, hats, jackets, coffee cups, lunchboxes, etc. They do the printing (only after someone has ordered the item) and split the profits with you. There are a couple of huge advantages to this arrangement: no inventory to store and no large investment.

As your company begins to build its' fanbase, you will need to sell merchandise at your shows. A lot of people purchase based on compulsion and not need. Your company will benefit by selling souvenirs of their evening. Mostly, in the indy ranks, wrestling companies sell the generic company t shirt. However, as your wrestlers gain notoriety, you may want to sell their t shirts based on how much interest and how large the following is of that athlete.

Think in terms of a snowball being pushed down a hill; The further you roll it, the larger it becomes. In a way, wrestling is all about momentum. Once you have merchandise selling at your shows and you have television, then you are able to sell your merchandise on your television show and also on your website. What can you sell on your website? Extra programs from previous shows, videos/DVDs, t-shirts, autographed photos and any wrestler gimmicks (if you can get Mick Foley on a card, I imagine you could sell a lot of dirty socks !) are all tempting acquisitions for a hungry fan.

You can also enlist other internet sites to help you with sales. Some indy promotions sell their tapes and merchandise on www.highspots.com. Although this has nothing to do with your company, Highspots has a tremendous selection of wrestling gear and masks (if any indy worker is interested).

Training schools are a popular addition to wrestling organizations. Although this might have been a more popular idea when there were more promotions seeking trained athletes, it might appeal to you to have home grown talent when you have achieved the goal of being on television. Many training schools work out of old garages and warehouses. You need to find a building that has a high ceiling in order to fully utilize your wrestling ring, i.e. you cannot jump from the top rope in a building with a low ceiling without avoiding a massive Excedrin headache. Also, a great advantage to having a training school is that if your building passes safety codes, you have an automatic venue to perform shows. Initially, you will not need to work hard to find places to rent.

Schools in this area charge as much as $6,000 per student for a two year training curriculum. A handful of trainees bring in a handful of money. There was one school in Southern California that grew so large that they had two training locations. Another way to bring in revenue from your training facility is to have fantasy camps where fans can come in for a day and see some of their favorite wrestlers.

Try to make contact with the WWE's talent relations (Bruce Pritchard and his brother Tom as of this writing). Invite them to your facilities and try to get them to allow your students to wrestle 'dark matches'. 'Dark matches' are a type of tryout that takes place at RAW and Smackdown events before the cameras begin to roll. You can contact the WWE by mail at: WWE, Attn: Talent Relations, 1241 East Main Street, Stamford, CT 06902.

There will always be peaks and valleys in this business. If things are a little dry today, that is no guarantee your school won't be overflowing tomorrow.

You can also rent your training ring to other wrestling companies. There are always up and coming organizations that will not have a ring. I've seen rings rented for approximately $750 to $800 and probably higher. Some businesses will rent your ring for advertising purposes. Make sure you are on the premises when others are using your ring so that damage will not be inflicted on it.

More exposure (good exposure) will bring more income. More income brings more opportunities.

Chapter 9

Time Limits: A few words about persistence and purpose

There are a certain number of businesses that will fail and a certain number that will succeed. The percentages are not in your favor. More businesses fail within the first couple of years than at any other period.

Be prudent in the things that you do so that you will not fail. Consider this your part-time income as you build your company. However, if you do fail in professional wrestling, it may not be the end of your dreams. If you really feel that this is what you need to do, you can rebuild and start anew.

I read as a young person that Abe Lincoln ran for office eight times. Just think if he would have quit on the eighth try! We would have been robbed of, arguably, our greatest president.

Also, keep in mind that your life is not defined by what you do but who you are.

Years ago, I used to read positive thinking books and hoped that they would energize me in my life. I will not write a long, boring story about my personal life but like everyone, I have had ups and downs. Positive thinking only lasts so long. Life has a way of tossing you around at times. That is inevitable.

The thing that I found that worked for me was a deeper strength that helps me every day. It's my faith and relationship with Jesus Christ. I understand what the Bible says when it talks about "the peace of God that passes understanding". My life is in order...even when there is chaos around me.

I'm finding that life is not about things because things have an emptiness to them if there isn't more to all of this. Don't get me wrong, I'm not much for religion or rituals or setting an impossible standard, but I've found that there is something deeper to my faith. It's rooted in love.

Whatever you find that works for you, that keeps you going, is where your strength needs to be. It's where your priorities should be, also. Everything that you hold onto is all that holds on to you. Remember, we do get older, jobs change, interests change, and as we've seen in wrestling, trends change. Wrestling won't comfort you when you are older, it won't give you a hug when you are lonely, it won't go to the movies with you on a Saturday night. Prioritize your life.

It's who you are not what you do. Don't let other people's opinions of you matter. Usually, those are rooted in jealousy.

Many promoters, like many businessmen, find their identity in wrestling. When they lose their promotion, they lose their identity. Your life should have a firmer foundation than that.

Before you begin in this career, I urge you to find out who you are, what your core values are, and what is most important to you. Your answers may surprise you. You may find out that you are getting involved in wrestling for all the wrong reasons. I did.

I may not know you personally but I do know that your Creator has given you unique and special talents. I wish for you success, prosperity and a personal knowledge of that Creator. Best of luck and don't ever give up!

Chapter 10

Closing Thoughts-Be a True Champion

Hopefully, I have conveyed the opinion that it's important to keep your business practices clean. Otherwise, your underhanded deals will be made public and you will lose the support of your much needed fans. Although wrestling seems to march on and survive countless scandals, a large number of promotions have fallen under their soiled names.

Treat wrestlers and fans with respect. Just because you can get away with shifty business practices, doesn't mean that you should. Remember, one mistake can ruin you and your business.

One of the biggest disgraces in wrestling, in my opinion, was the introduction of hardcore or extreme wrestling. This type of wrestling often uses barbed wire, glass, thumbtacks, burning tables and other creative yet hazardous stunts. Backyard wrestling, which usually exists of little or no wrestling moves like its' extreme counterpart, is an imitation of many of the ridiculous and dangerous stunts used in hardcore wrestling. This style has seriously injured wrestlers and killed backyard imitators (kids killed way too young for no sane reason). Some of the blame might be the parents who do not enforce proper discipline in their children but a lot of blame falls on the so called professionals.

As of this writing, bay area wrestling is pretty much the same with the exception of APW. There was recently a lawsuit filed in response to a tragic death at their training facility. The family of the deceased student is suing based on a charge of negligence.

Also, many smaller wrestling companies are cropping up in the bay area. I wish them all the best of luck. On a larger scale, the WWE's ratings have been lackluster in early 2003.

Mark Anderson, the person who introduced me to this sport, left wrestling two years ago. Then, during the original release of this book, he was back with a wrestling school in Eastern Canada. This promotion would be co-owned with Jim "The Anvil" Neidhart and Dan "The Beast" Severn. Their school and promotion was called Canadian Extreme Wrestling. Their web address is www.cxwwrestling.com.

Unfortunately, their first show was canceled due to financial issues. Several months went by and the last I heard from Mark, the CXW was not close to being re-opened. I wish Mark the best because he is a great person and without that chance meeting with Mark, I would not have met Ric Drasin, Mike Modest, Ryan Timm, the Honky Tonk Man or anyone else I've had the opportunity to meet.

Ok, it's Mark's fault I met Kirk White and Roland Alexander, too. I guess we're even.

I suspect you all know that Ric Drasin is still active in wrestling, acting and various other ventures. The guy doesn't quit. He has several movies in the works.

My mom and my two brothers are still related to me.

As stated before, wrestling runs hot and cold. So, you really never know what is around the corner. One thing that I believe is certain, wrestling will always be in the fabric of American culture.

I was helping Mike Modest and Donovan Morgan promote their company, Pro Wrestling Iron, but during the time of this revision (for Ric's book), I decided to take a break. I have a webpage, www.BruceDCollins.com. You can reach me at BColl95478@aol.com. I would be happy and honored to hear from you.

Remember, intelligence will not guarantee success. Luck

won't do it, either. The only thing I have found that gives me consistent achievement is something I call P.P. I believe in patient persistence.

Take care of yourself.

Bruce

PS. As I make the finishing touches on this book, the unbelievable has happened. APW and BTW are promoting a show together! Kirk White and Roland Alexander will never change.

970915

Made in the USA